The *Sh*adows Behind Me

THE AZRIELI SERIES OF HOLOCAUST SURVIVOR MEMOIRS: PREVIOUSLY PUBLISHED TITLES

The Shadows Behind Me

Willie Sterner

The Azrieli Foundation
www.azrielifoundation.org

Cover and book design by Mark Goldstein
Endpaper maps by Martin Gilbert
Inside maps by François Blanc

LIBRARY AND ARCHIVES CANADA CATALOGUING IN PUBLICATION

Sterner, Willie, 1919–
        The shadows behind me / Willie Sterner.

(The Azrieli series of Holocaust survivor memoirs ; 3)
Includes bibliographical references and index.
ISBN 978-1-897470-18-3

1. Sterner, Willie, 1919–. 2. Holocaust, Jewish (1939–1945) – Poland – Personal narratives. 3. Holocaust survivors – Canada –Biography. 4. Polish Canadians – Biography. I. Azrieli Foundation II. Title. III. Series: Azrieli series of Holocaust survivor memoirs 3

DS134.72.S85A3 2010   940.53'18092   C2010-905772-4

PRINTED IN CANADA

The Azrieli Series of Holocaust Survivor Memoirs

Contents

Series Preface:
In their own words...

In telling these stories, the writers have liberated themselves. For so many years we did not speak about it, even when we became free people living in a free society. Now, when at last we are writing about what happened to us in this dark period of history, knowing that our stories will be read and live on, it is possible for us to feel truly free. These unique historical documents put a face on what was lost, and allow readers to grasp the enormity of what happened to six million Jews – one story at a time.

David J. Azrieli, C.M., C.Q., M.Arch
Holocaust survivor and founder, The Azrieli Foundation

Since the end of World War II, over 30,000 Jewish Holocaust survivors have immigrated to Canada. Who they are, where they came from, what they experienced and how they built new lives for themselves and their families are important parts of our Canadian heritage. The Azrieli Foundation's Holocaust Survivor Memoirs Program was established to preserve and share the memoirs written by those who survived the twentieth-century Nazi genocide of the Jews of Europe and later made their way to Canada. The program is guided by the conviction that each survivor of the Holocaust has a remarkable story to tell, and that such stories play an important role in education about tolerance and diversity.

Millions of individual stories are lost to us forever. By preserving the stories written by survivors and making them widely available to a broad audience, the Azrieli Series of Holocaust Survivor Memoirs seeks to sustain the memory of all those who perished at the hands of hatred, abetted by indifference and apathy. The personal accounts of those who survived against all odds are as different as the people who wrote them, but all demonstrate the courage, strength, wit and luck that it took to prevail and survive in such terrible adversity. The memoirs are also moving tributes to people – strangers and friends – who risked their lives to help others, and who, through acts of kindness and decency in the darkest of moments, frequently helped the persecuted maintain faith in humanity and courage to endure. These accounts offer inspiration to all, as does the survivors' desire to share their experiences so that new generations can learn from them.

The Holocaust Survivor Memoirs Program collects, archives and publishes these distinctive records and the print editions are available free of charge to libraries, educational institutions and Holocaust-education programs across Canada, and to the general public at Azrieli Foundation educational events. Online editions of the books are available free of charge on our web site, www.azrielifoundation.org.

The Azrieli Foundation would like to express appreciation to the following people for their invaluable efforts in producing this series: Mary Arvanitakis, Josée Bégaud, Florence Buathier, Franklin Carter, Mark Celinscack, Darrel Dickson (Maracle Press), Andrea Geddes Poole, Sir Martin Gilbert, Pascale Goulias-Didiez, Stan Greenspan, Karen Helm, Carson Phillips, Pearl Saban, Jody Spiegel, Erika Tucker, Lise Viens, and Margie Wolfe and Emma Rodgers of Second Story Press.

Introduction

Willie Sterner's remarkable account of life in wartime Poland illustrates the incredible resilience of the human spirit. From the moment the Germans invaded his homeland in September 1939 until his liberation by the Americans in May 1945, he met each new challenge – and there were many, to be sure – with courage and determination. Sterner was a painter by trade who had learned his skills as a young man working for his father's company. Painting served a dual purpose for Sterner during the war. Not only did it help him to survive his terrible six-year ordeal – even the notorious commandant of the Płaszów forced labour camp seemed to appreciate his painting skills – but his passion for his trade also helped him hold onto some shred of human dignity in the inhumane and degrading environment that the Nazis created. Painting reminded him of his family, which meant everything to Sterner, and even at his lowest point, when he was in complete shock and shattered by the deliberate murder of his family in the summer and fall of 1942, he still did not give up and somehow found the strength to carry on. Courage and tenacity characterize Sterner's life.

Born into an observant and close-knit Jewish family the year after World War I ended, Willie Sterner spent the first decade of his life in Wolbrom, Poland, a small town just north of Krakow. In 1928, his father, who was also a painter by trade, moved his large and growing family to Krakow. Sterner recalls with joy his coming of age and, by his own admission, he had a normal and happy childhood growing up in Poland.

In the heart of east-central Europe, Poland had long been an important centre of Jewish migration and culture and in the interwar years it was home to the largest Jewish community in Europe. The years between the two world wars, some argue, mark a high point or golden age in Polish and Polish-Jewish history. After 150 years of its territory being partitioned between Russia, Prussia and Austria, Poland was liberated from foreign rule and recognized as an independent state in 1919, the same year that Willie Sterner was born.[1] Poland's rebirth was not so easy, though, and in the years immediately following independence it struggled to become a nation-state. The Russians were unhappy about Polish independence and for two years fought the Poles for control of the borderlands between the two countries. The issue was finally resolved on March 18, 1921, when Poland and Russia signed the Treaty of Riga that officially defined Poland's eastern frontier.

Territorial settlements were the least of Poland's worries, however. In order to build a viable nation-state, it was also crucial for the newly independent country to create its own political, economic and social institutions. The Entente powers of Great Britain, France and, beginning in 1917, the United States, had fought for the right to national self-determination and pledged their support, but once independence was granted to the fledgling democracies of east-central Europe, they were offered little in the way of tangible help and were pretty much left to fend for themselves. Some states seemed to

---

1   The United States was the first of the Entente powers to recognize Poland as an independent state on January 22, 1919. Willie Sterner was born nine months later on September 15.

have an easier time than others developing democratic institutions. Poland struggled most, not only because it lacked support from the West, but also because of its geography – it was a country sandwiched between two revisionist and increasingly hostile states – Germany and Russia – making it politically (and physically) vulnerable. Border disputes coupled with years of occupation also meant that Poland was not an ethnically pure nation-state. In fact, it was home to sizable minority groups, including large numbers of Germans, Lithuanians, Ukrainians and, of course, 3.3 million Ashkenazi Jews. Unlike its neighbour Czechoslovakia, Poland struggled with establishing democratic processes and power-sharing within and among the various minority groups that made up 30 per cent of its interwar population. Despite all these problems, Willie Sterner and other Polish Jews remember their youth in Poland with great fondness.

Sterner's nostalgia for this era should not be surprising – the 1939-1945 period brought with it not only the total destruction of his family but the violent end to Polish-Jewish civilization and history as it had existed for centuries. Was Jewish life in interwar Poland in fact, as many scholars have asked, good for the Jews?[2] The answer, not surprisingly, is mixed. There is no question that interwar Poland gave birth to some of the most important ideologies and political movements of modern Jewish history. The Zionist movement, for instance, dominated the political landscape in the interwar period and Sterner's own father was a committed member of Jabotinsky's Brigade. Sterner himself recalls his own membership in Akiva, a Zionist youth organization. The Bundists – Jewish socialists – also flourished in the years before World War II. The Bund was an organization that not

---

2   Ezra Mendelsohn describes interwar Poland as being in a kind of "manic-depressive" state, oscillating between euphoric highs and depressive lows. See idem, "Jewish politics in interwar Poland: An overview," in Yisrael Gutman and Jehuda Reinharz (eds.), *The Jews of Poland between Two World Wars* (Hanover and London: University Press of New England, 1989), 9–19.

only fought for "equal rights for the Jewish minority in Poland" but also demanded "cultural, personal, and administrative autonomy."[3] Culturally, Polish Jewry thrived in the interwar period, producing an unparalleled number of performances in theatre, an enormous number of published books and a vital Yiddish press that had a wide circulation among the literate and politicized Polish Jewish community. Along with this renaissance, however, interwar Poland also gave rise to an increasingly virulent form of political antisemitism. While scholars debate the significance of interwar Polish antisemitism as a factor in the Holocaust, Sterner clearly remembers isolated incidents of bullying and hatred, although his overall recollections are of happy times.[4]

The outbreak of the war immediately changed everything. On September 1, 1939, the Germans invaded Poland and five days later they occupied Krakow, which became the seat of the German Civil Administration of the *Generalgouvernement* – the territory in central Poland that was conquered by the Germans but not annexed to the Third Reich – under the leadership of Hans Frank. As the Holocaust in Poland unfolded, Sterner and his family became victims of Nazi anti-Jewish policies that became more and more violent. Almost as soon as the war broke out, Sterner and his brothers were forced to work for the Germans, with no pay and no food, but luckily were allowed to return to their family each night. In 1941, in an attempt to mitigate their suffering, his father moved the family back to Wolbrom, where the young Sterner worked as a painter. While things were not ideal, they were better than they had been in Krakow and staying together as a family was very important to them; even if they lacked basic provisions, they drew strength from being together. In

---

3   Abraham Brumberg, "The Bund and the Polish Socialist Party in the late 1930s," in Gutman and Reinharz (eds.), 75–76.

4   Yisrael Gutman, "Polish Antisemitism between the wars: An overview," in Gutman and Reinharz (eds.), 97–108.

the summer of 1942, the situation worsened when the Nazis began their murderous campaign against Polish Jewry – which came to be known as the "Final Solution" – and deportations from Poland's ghettos began in earnest. In the first week of June alone, 7,000 Jews were deported from the ghetto in Krakow to Belzec, a death camp not far from Lublin, where approximately half a million Polish Jews were murdered in less than one year. Sterner's family did not escape the violence. In the late summer of 1942, the Jews of Wolbrom were rounded up and his mother and four sisters were put on a cattle car and deported to Treblinka. He never saw them again. He and his brothers and father were sent to the ghetto in Krakow where they survived until October, when the rest of his family (his father and two brothers) were murdered in an *Aktion*, a violent roundup of Jews that more often than not resulted in murder. Following the death of his father and brothers Sterner left the place where he was hiding and was captured. He spent the remainder of the war as a slave labourer.

In *The Shadows Behind Me*, Willie Sterner's memoir of his six-year ordeal as a slave labourer during the Nazi occupation of Poland (1939–1945), the episode that particularly stands out is the one that demonstrates Sterner's genuine affection and admiration for Oskar Schindler and the role that the Nazi businessman played in his survival. Despite the fact that Sterner's name does not appear amid the 1,098 people on Oskar Schindler's now-famous list of rescued Jews, indeed, as Sterner writes, Schindler was his "hero." Not only did he restore Sterner's health and confidence by giving him meaningful work for a time, but in doing so, he also represented hope in a near-hopeless situation.

Fortunately for Sterner, Schindler's nearby Deutsche Emailwaren Fabrik (DEF) was devoted to creating enamelware for the Nazi war effort and in the spring of 1943, Schindler gave the young Sterner a job as a painter in his Emalia factory. Because he was so good at his trade, Schindler also made him his personal art painter and for a year Sterner lived and worked at Emalia. When the Soviet Red Army was approaching Krakow in the late summer of 1944, however, Schindler prepared to move his factory and as many of its Jewish workers as he could to his hometown of Brünnlitz, Moravia, in the present-day Czech Republic. Unfortunately, Sterner did not make it onto the final list of those who would be protected.[5] Instead he was sent back to Płaszów, the slave labour camp in the suburbs of Krakow under the control of the notoriously brutal Commandant Amon Göth. Even there, where so many perished at the whim of Göth, Willie Sterner had utilized his painting skills for survival. The last year of the war wreaked havoc on the Nazi concentration camp system and, as was frequently the case, prisoners who could still work were forced to move from camp to camp further and further behind German lines. Thousands of them died in the transfer process.

Willie Sterner was one such prisoner who was moved from camp to camp. From Płaszów he was sent by cattle car to Mauthausen in Austria. Three weeks later he was sent to the infamous Gusen II, a subcamp of Mauthausen, where German jet planes were assembled in an underground facility and where the fumes from painting the planes nearly killed him. In mid-April 1945, as the war was drawing to a close, he marched sixty kilometres from Gusen to Gunskirchen, along with the remaining prisoners who were still alive. In indescribable pain and nearly dead from starvation when he arrived, Sterner was liberated somewhat unceremoniously from the Austrian camp by American troops on May 5, 1945, two days before Admiral Karl Dönitz officially surrendered to the Allies. Though Sterner barely survived the last year of the war, he does not blame Schindler for his ordeal; in fact, he has nothing but the highest regard for the man he describes as the "saviour and protector" of the Jewish people, illus-

----

5   There is evidence to suggest that Schindler did not decide who would and would not get onto the list.

trating the complex relationship between the Nazi businessman and those whose lives he touched.

Literally at the end of his reserves and lucky to be alive, Sterner walked away from Gunskirchen and never looked back. Refusing to feel sorry for himself, when the director of the United Nations relief organization asked him to organize a Jewish police force in the Wels DP camp, he jumped at the chance because, as he tells us, it was good for him to "keep busy." He became chief of the Jewish police first in Wels and then in Linz-Bindermichl, Austria and in the process started to rebuild his life and regain his dignity. Sterner spent three years in Austria after the war. In an attempt to start fresh, he made his way to Canada in October 1948 with his wife, Eva, whom he had first met during the death march from Gusen to Gunskirchen and married in Salzburg, Austria in the summer of 1946. Having survived six years of hell and three years of uncertainty, Willie and Eva put down roots in Montreal and made a new life for themselves. It was not easy for them. Willie worked hard as a painter for a number of years before eventually opening his own painting company and, with Eva, raised their two sons. Today, she and Willie travel regularly, volunteer with Holocaust centres in the United States and Canada and remain close to their children and grandchildren. Closeness to family, Willie candidly notes at the end of his memoir, is "the best medicine for survivors."

~

Whenever I teach the History of the Holocaust to university students, I always ask my class to read a number of survivor memoirs and answer the question, "How should we understand the survivor experience?" Without fail, students talk about "luck" as an important factor in survival – not surprising since virtually every survivor from Primo Levi to Ruth Klüger and Elie Wiesel raise the issue. In *The Shadows Behind Me*, Willie Sterner tells us repeatedly that he was lucky. He was indeed lucky that he was such a good painter and that the many people he encountered during the war – from the beneficent Oskar Schindler to the sadistic Amon Göth, all appreciated his skill. In the end, you could say that luck *and* painting saved Willie Sterner's life.

Hilary Earl
Nipissing University
2010

POLAND

LITHUANIA

EAST PRUSSIA
(GERMANY)

GERMANY

Berlin

Vistula

Warsaw

P O L A N D

Wolbrom

Pustków

U S S R

Prague

C Z E C H O S L O V A K I A

Krakow

Dębica

Vienna

—— Borders in 1937

© 2010 - The Azrieli Foundation

KRAKOW AND SURROUNDINGS

Krakow Airport

Rakowice Camp

Vistula

Krakow

Deutsche Emailwaren Fabrik

Jewish Ghetto

Plaszów

5 km

© 2010 - The Azrieli Foundation

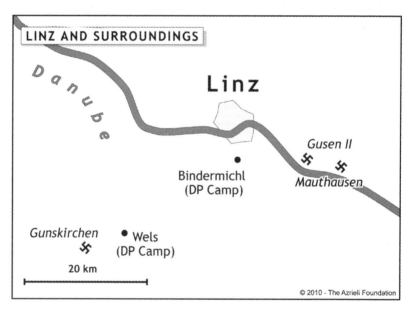

I dedicate this memoir to my loved ones who perished in the Holocaust.

I will always remember them.

I will never forget my non-Jewish friends – among them the Strzalka family – who risked their lives to save Jews. I am particularly grateful to my heroes Oskar Schindler and Kazimiera Strzalka – Righteous Among the Nations.

I am also indebted to the many Jewish people, including members of the Jewish Immigrant Aid Society, who helped me and my wife when we came to Canada.

Author's Preface

The murder of six million innocent Jews by the Nazis during World War II wasn't accidental. It was planned by the Nazi German government, professors, lawyers and other highly educated Germans. The Nazi terror machine gave the Germans a free hand to go into Jewish homes, take all Jewish valuables and murder Jewish families. The victims of these crimes were chosen only because they were born into the Jewish faith. When the Nazis and their collaborators began their mass murder and destruction of defenceless Jewish families, world and church leaders were silent. They did little or nothing to help the Jews.

I am the only survivor of a loving family of nine. I lost my parents, two younger brothers and four younger sisters in the Holocaust. I will never forget the horrible time in 1942 in Poland when – paralyzed – I stood and watched my dear family harassed and destroyed by Nazi murderers. It has been very painful for me to write down my memories, but I had no choice. It is my duty as a survivor to tell the whole world about the Holocaust and my tragedy and the six million *keddoshim* (holy ones).

I now work for the Holocaust Centre in Montreal, Quebec, and the Holocaust Documentation and Education Center in Miami Beach, Florida. I speak on TV and to newspaper reporters. I also speak in synagogues, churches, community centres, high schools, colleges, universities and other organizations. Our duty as survivors is to work hard to fight all hatemongers and antisemitic organizations. Hatred and prejudice are dangers to all people.

I am pleased with my work. The students I meet are very interested in the Holocaust and promise to educate their families and friends. I hope that our work with young people will help to fight hatred and prejudice against Jews and other innocent minorities. I hope that Jews will be united and successful in that same fight against hatred and prejudice. I look to our governments to be more helpful in our fight for justice.

~

A Holocaust survivor is an actor. We try to act like other people, especially in front of family and friends, but the truth is that we never will be. The terrible memories of what we experienced and what we have lost are always with us. On holidays and special occasions, we feel the absence of loved ones who should be there to share the simcha with us. At night, the terror and pain becomes inescapable. We try not to show what we feel to our children but they cannot help but be affected by our pain. The wounds are deep in our hearts; we are haunted by the shadows behind us.

Life in Wolbrom and Krakow

I was born into a loving and happy Jewish family in Wolbrom, Poland, on September 15, 1919. My father, Hersz Leib Sterner, was an honest, hard-working tradesman, and my mother, Hinda Reizel Sterner, took care of our family at home. I was the oldest of seven children.

Wolbrom was a small town of 7,000 with a Jewish population of just over 4,000. Outside the town there were two large forests and a small riverbank. In town there was an electric company owned by a Jewish man named Mr. Neier and two large factories: an enamel factory that produced pots and pans and a rubber factory that produced other household goods. We had a volunteer fire department, public schools, synagogues, bet hamidrashes (religious schools) and cheders (Jewish elementary schools). We had Zionist and Jewish socialist organizations.[1] We even had a Jewish, Yiddish-language theatre, where my father was an amateur actor.[2] Before World War II, everyone in

---

1 A number of significant Jewish political movements flourished in Poland from the late nineteenth century to the outbreak of World War II. For more information on Zionist and Jewish socialist movements in interwar Poland, see the glossary.

2 The Yiddish language was spoken by a majority of Jews in East-Central Europe. It is derived from Middle High German with elements of Hebrew, Aramaic, Romance and Slavic languages, and is written in Hebrew characters. There are similarities between Yiddish and contemporary German.

our area had to work very hard because most families were large – the husband was usually the sole breadwinner and the wife had the big job of taking care of the family. People had to be very frugal – some people took *kotry* (peat) from the wet fields, dried it out and burned it instead of coal because it was much cheaper. But our lives were happy because we lived according to our Jewish traditions, and we appreciated our families and our good friends.

We loved our small town of Wolbrom, but the pace of life was slow, so a lot of our young people moved to larger cities such as Warsaw, Krakow, Sosnowiec and Lodz. In 1928, my father decided to move our family to the beautiful city of Krakow, forty kilometres south of Wolbrom, where there were more opportunities for work and a better education. City life was different, more open and progressive. It was a very good move for us.

Krakow is a historic city on the Vistula River in the south of Poland. For three hundred years, from the beginning of the fourteenth century to the beginning of the seventeenth century, Krakow was the capital of Poland and the Wawel Palace, the home of former Polish kings, is located there. The city has many large parks and gardens such as Błonia, Planty and Krzemionki. It is a city of sports clubs, theatres, restaurants and churches.

By 1931, the Jewish residents of Krakow numbered about 55,000 of the city's overall population of 215,000. Centred largely in the Kazimierz district, Krakow's Jewish community was one of the oldest in Europe. Jews worked as professors, doctors, pharmacists, rabbis, cantors, publishers, manufacturers and tradesmen. We lived in the Podgórze district, which was very mixed – Jews and Poles and people from other countries all lived and worked side by side. There were many Jewish communal institutions in Krakow that reflected the variations in the community. Jews read daily newspapers in Polish, Yiddish and Hebrew. Some read the daily Zionist newspaper and attended Zionist conferences – Zionist youth movements, in particular, were very strong in the city. For education, there were cheders, bet hamidrashes and the Hebrew gymnasium (high school). The members of the Jewish community worshipped in both the more liberal or Reform temples, such as the Mizrachi and Kupa synagogues, and in Orthodox shuls such as the Izaak, the Alte and the Remuh.[3] Krakow also had a Jewish, Yiddish-language theatre and a hospital that was organized and run by Jews, although the patients came from all parts of the community.

In the years before 1939, most Jews strictly observed their religion and maintained Jewish traditions – even Jews who weren't very religious followed tradition. For example, we all kept kosher homes.[4] On Friday afternoons, before the Sabbath, we closed our businesses, cleaned our houses and dressed in our best clothes.[5] Each family put a white tablecloth and a candelabra with candles on the table and the whole family gathered together. Sometimes we had a guest for the Sabbath – that was also a Jewish tradition. Then, on Saturday morning, we all went to the synagogue for Sabbath services. Afterward we came home for a special holiday meal: gefilte fish and delicious *cholent*.[6]

I attended Sabbath services in the temple at 24 Miodowa Street. Built as a progressive Liberal Reform synagogue (Postepowa synagoga) in 1862, it featured a beautiful choir and geometrical images of plants and animals in thirty-six stained-glass windows. Rabbis de-

---

3 For more information on Reform and Orthodox Judaism, see the glossary.

4 Observant Jews follow a system of rules known as *kashruth*, or kosher dietary laws. These rules regulate what observant Jews eat, how food is prepared and how meat and poultry are slaughtered. For more information on the definition of kosher, see the glossary.

5 The Jewish Sabbath, or Shabbat, begins at sunset on Friday and ends at sundown on Saturday. For more information on Jewish Sabbath traditions, see the glossary.

6 Gefilte fish is a dish made of chopped whitefish that is formed into patties and then boiled and *cholent* is a traditional slow-cooked meat, bean and vegetable stew. Both are often eaten at the festive Shabbat lunch on Saturdays and on Jewish holidays.

livered weekly sermons in Polish and German. Dr. Ozjasz Yehoshua Thon – one of the organizers of the first Zionist Congress in 1897 and the leader of the Jewish political party who sat in the Polish parliament – delivered sermons there until his death in 1936. I loved to attend the Sabbath services in our temple.

In Krakow – not only in Kazimierz but all over the city – the observance of Jewish holidays and traditions was evident all around us. Hasidim wore their silk black overcoats, and some wore fur hats (called a *shtreimel* in Yiddish) and white socks.[7] In Jewish religious law, it is forbidden to use electricity or to make a fire in our ovens on holy days, including the Sabbath, so we would ask our Christian-Polish neighbours to light our homes and heat the ovens. We gave each person a piece of challah – the traditional braided egg bread eaten on the Sabbath – and ten groszy (ten cents).

Another holiday, Purim, was a joyful and special celebration.[8] We always had a beautiful parade on the streets of Kazimierz, called an Adloyada, with lively Purim shows on the platforms of the large trucks. Everyone, especially families, had a really good time.

～

My father started a contracting company under the name of Fine Home Painting, Decorating and Sign Painting (the name in Polish was the Zakland Malarski pokojowy szyldowy lakierniczy). He represented the Wolfrum company of Vienna for paint, décor supplies and designs, and also sold drapes, towels, oil cloths, tablecloths and domestic supplies. My father's dream was to have his own paint store with the name "Sterner and Sons." We had already acquired a lot of

---

7   Hasidism is a Jewish spiritual movement that stresses piety and joyful prayer. For more information, see the glossary.

8   Purim is a holiday that commemorates the Jews' escape from annihilation in ancient Persia. It is marked by carnivals and parades in which children masquerade as figures from the Purim story. For more information, see the glossary.

merchandise, found a good location for the store and were ready to open when the Nazis took away my father's dream – and my dream too.

My father was a devoted family man and a loving husband – our family was the most important thing in his life. Honest and smart, he worked hard at his trade to provide for our family. He loved acting in the amateur musical productions at the Jewish theatre and he was very good at it. He was also talented in singing traditional Jewish songs. My father was a proud Jew and a strong Zionist who dreamed of moving to Israel with our family. He was a member of the Brit HaChayal (Jabotinsky's Brigade).[9] He gave us a lot of love, and our family loved him very much in return.

My mother worked very hard at taking care of our family – looking after the household, keeping her children well dressed and clean and preparing the most wonderful traditional Jewish foods for us. Unfortunately, she wasn't in the best of health – she suffered from arthritis and every year my father sent her to the spa town of Busko-Zdrój, known for its medicinal waters, for a month. It helped a little. But even though her daily routine started at six o'clock in the morning and ended at eleven at night, she never complained that she was ill or tired. My mother was content watching her children grow up happy and healthy.

My parents were the best anyone could wish for. They dedicated their lives to our family, doing everything they could to keep our family cheerful and together. They were also good to their friends and neighbours.

---

9 The Brit HaChayal (Union of Soldiers or Revisionist Army Veteran's Association) was established in 1933 as an arm of Revisionist Zionism that advocated Jewish self-defence and self-determination. It was closely modelled on the teachings of Ze'ev Jabotinsky, who founded the Revisionist Zionist movement and strongly supported the establishment of a Jewish state in Palestine. For more information on Jabotinsky and Revisionist Zionism, see the glossary.

I finished seven grades of public school before going to work for my father's company, painting and decorating houses, as well as doing some art painting. In Poland before World War II, children went to public schools until they were fourteen years of age. That was the law. Afterward they went to a high school or college if the parents were wealthy and could afford to pay the high price. If recent graduates couldn't afford higher education, they had to learn a trade. I loved my trade – it was interesting and I liked working for my father. He was talented and knew a great deal about all forms of decorative painting. I also worked for other painting contractors in Krakow, Sosnowiec, Katowice and Olkusz, so I continued to gain knowledge and experience. I then went to a technical school for three years and learned about estimating, painting, contracting and art painting. The diploma I received when I finished the program made it possible for me to apply for a contractor's licence.

While I was attending technical school I also had to go to pre-military school two days a week as part of my required preparation for compulsory military service. I liked military life; I learned about the military and gained a great deal of self-discipline and self-esteem. My classmates and I graduated from the technical school and the pre-military school at the same time; this was in 1937, when I was eighteen. At the graduation ceremony, we got our diplomas and had a military parade in front of Mayor Mieczyslaw Kaplicki of Krakow, General Bernard Mond of the Krakow 6th infantry division, local governor Michal Roch Gnoiński and other dignitaries. I was given the privilege of choosing which military unit I would serve in as a volunteer until I turned twenty-one and twice went to military camps on manoeuvres. I really enjoyed the experience.

My younger brother Josel Meier – he was two years younger than me, born in 1922 – started out working as a housepainter in my father's company, but he never did learn the trade. He didn't want to be a housepainter but didn't want to hurt our father's feelings and professional pride. My father could tell, however, that Josel Meier would never be a good painter and instead registered him in a design school for *trykot* (knitwear). Josel Meier liked the school very much. He was an honest, good-natured young man, an intellectual who loved books. As a member of the Maccabi Jewish sports club, he played soccer and ping-pong, and went ice skating. Josel was a proud young man, a wonderful son and brother with a lot of close friends.

My next-youngest brother, Abraham, two years younger than Josel Meier, born in 1924, was exceptionally bright. When he was registered to go into Grade 1 in public school, he ended up being ill for most of the school year and couldn't attend. Fortunately, his health improved three months before the end of the school year, so my father asked the principal if he could send Abraham to class as an observer. The principal was a friend of my father's, so he readily gave his permission, but cautioned my father, "Don't expect Abraham to be an active student in the last three months of the school year. There isn't enough time for him to make up what he's missed; Abraham should only sit and listen." Whenever the teacher asked questions in class, however, my brother could never sit there quietly – he was always the first student to give the right answer and impressed his teacher with what he already knew. By the end of the year, Abraham had earned the marks to enter Grade 2.

From the time he was very young, Abraham bought all kinds of used watch parts from a watchmaker with whatever small change he had and constructed tiny moving machines, miniature cars and other structures. He even made blueprints. Abraham was always so busy that he had little time for fun and no time to visit his friends, so his friends came to our home to watch him create his little machines. All his friends were proud of him and admired his beautiful creations. They really understood him and appreciated his talents. Abraham was well-loved by his family, his teachers and his friends.

One summer, Abraham attended a Jewish day camp sponsored by a philanthropic organization in Krakow that was headed by a prominent man named Mr. Rabinowicz. During a visit to the camp, Mr.

Rabinowicz decided to join the children for lunch and sat down at one of the long tables. Abraham, who was sitting across from him, took a piece of paper and a pencil out of his pocket and drew his portrait. My brother was a shy boy, so, when he finished the drawing, he put it into his pocket. His friend, however, pulled it out and gave it to Mr. Rabinowicz, who was very surprised and asked, "Who made this beautiful portrait of me?" When my brother's friend pointed to him, Mr. Rabinowicz called Abraham over, asked for his name and address and told him, "Keep up your nice work! You have the talent to be a good artist."

My brother didn't say anything about the incident when he came home from camp; to him, it just wasn't a big deal. A few days later, though, Mr. Rabinowicz came to our home at Zamoyskiego 10 to speak to my parents. He said that Abraham should go to art school and that he had the potential to become a great artist; he even offered to pay for Abraham's tuition and all expenses while he went to high school and art school until he was ready to become a professional artist. My parents were thrilled with Mr. Rabinowicz's generous offer and only too happy to accept. They were very proud of my brother and knew that this was a once-in-a-lifetime chance for him to get a higher education. Even though my father was a good provider, there were seven children in our family and higher education in Poland was expensive. This wonderful gift was the best news we had had in a long time and we were all excited about Abraham's prospects for the future.

Abraham had to take an intelligence test to make sure that he had potential in areas other than art. The test results showed that Abraham had a high level of skill in science and physics as well as art. In 1938, he became a proud student at the Hebrew high school in Krakow. The principal and the teachers were pleased with his performance – he was such an excellent student that he gave lessons to other students during his free time, even ones in the higher grades. Mr. Rabinowicz's plan was that Abraham would finish the Hebrew high school in Krakow and then go to university in Jerusalem.

Abraham was so talented that nothing was too hard for him. He played a number of musical instruments – the piano, violin and drums – and had a professional-quality violin at home that he loved to play often. His friend's father was a musical conductor who owned a lot of musical instruments and Abraham was permitted to play them whenever he was free from schoolwork. Abraham was truly a genius.

My younger sisters Ida, Genia and Rachel attended public school. They were all lovely girls, good students, and fine daughters and sisters. Ida, who was born in 1926, was a great help to our mother with the housework. She loved everything about school – the homework and her teachers – and during her free time, she loved to read books, write short poems and sew clothing for dolls. She was happy and had lots of good friends.

Genia, born in 1927, liked to sing traditional Jewish songs with our father. She had a lovely voice and we all enjoyed listening to her singing. She liked to draw pictures and we called her our "small artist." Genia also helped my mother at home. She was an easy-going child with a beautiful smile.

Rachel, born in 1929, was a more serious young person – she was always thinking and reading books, and, like Ida, she loved school. She was always ready to help our mother at home because she knew that our mother wasn't in the best of health. Rachel had a lot of friends and she was sweet to everyone.

My youngest sister, Sarah, born in 1932, was a delight to our family and was spoiled by all of us. She was only six years old when the war began, too young to attend school, but she pretended that she was a schoolgirl and did "homework" like her sisters. Sarah was always ready to take part in family discussions and singing. Like Genia, she was a happy child with a big smile and lots of friends.

My parents loved us all and were proud of us. We all – my parents, my brothers, my sisters – loved each other very much. I miss them all terribly and will never forget them.

⁓

Jews had lived in Poland for more than six hundred years, but Polish nationalism, religious differences and general mistrust on both sides meant that life with our Polish neighbours wasn't always friendly. The majority of Poles were Catholics, and the Church exerted a strong influence in Poland generally. Jewish culture was very different from that of our Polish Catholic neighbours. Jews didn't often socialize with Poles; but, as I've said, we did live together and work together.

As I've mentioned, we were forbidden to use electricity on holidays such as the Sabbath, so we had to ask our Polish neighbours to help out in return for a piece of challah and a little money. Perhaps when these Poles came into our homes and saw a table set with a white tablecloth and a candelabra, and saw Jews wearing clothes that were nicer than their own weekly clothing, even though the Jewish family of five might be living in a one-room apartment, they thought that all Jews were rich. They might not have realized that many Jewish families didn't eat any meat all week in order to save money to buy a chicken for the Sabbath or the high holidays. It was a common misconception among ordinary Poles that all Jews were very rich. I remember that some Poles used to say that to Jews, "Polish money is kosher, but the goy (non-Jew) is *treif* (not kosher)."

For many people, the dislike between Jews and Poles was mutual. Some punks would shout "Jew" at us as if it was a derogatory word, but I had no problem with it – I was a proud Jew. The Hasidic Jews were particular targets because of their pious behaviour and distinctive look – they wore full beards and *peyes* (long, curled sidelocks). For their part, some Jews called Polish people "goy," "shegetz" and "shiksa" – all derogatory terms for non-Jews. And if a Polish person disagreed with a Jew over some issue, the Pole was often branded an antisemite by the Jew. But in our home we were more open-minded and friendly with our Polish neighbours. My father's philosophy was that the most important rule for any person's behaviour was that he or she should strive to be decent and honest. In general, we tried to be good neighbours. We did work together with the Poles and we did business with them. Still, the atmosphere was often divisive, neither healthy nor friendly.

There was an antisemitic organization in Krakow called the Endeks.[10] They were only mildly threatening – they didn't take any direct action against us or harm us and they didn't seem to have any specific goals. We sometimes had little skirmishes with them, but most of the time we proudly stood up to them. When I was growing up, most Jews weren't brought up to fight or defend themselves. We had a saying that "It's not nice for a Jewish boy to fight; it's nice for them (meaning the Poles)." When young Polish punks wanted to have fun, they would stop a Hasidic Jew on the street, call him names and give him a little push. The Jewish man wouldn't fight back; he would run away as fast as he could. Despite the shame they felt at being taunted, it was considered even more shameful for Jewish men – especially religiously observant Jews – to fight to defend themselves; a lot of Jews walked with their heads down and some of the punks had a really good time. A few young Jewish men who were less traditional were willing to stand up to the punks and fight for their pride and dignity. Those Jews got respect, but there weren't too many of them. I, for one, was proud of them. Not my father, though – he always said that we should be proud Jews without putting anyone else down.

There were also a number of anti-Jewish measures passed by the Polish government. In 1936, Prime Minister Składkowski made it clear to the Polish people – and especially to the hoodlums – that although he didn't support physical attacks against the Jews, he encouraged economic measures against them.[11] So some of the young

---

10 For more information on the Endeks, see the glossary.

11 In a 1936 speech in the Polish parliament, Prime Minister Składkowski argued in favour of economic boycotts of Jewish businesses, preference given to Poles for loans and encouraging Poles to move their businesses into predominantly Jewish areas.

punks stood in front of Jewish stores and tried to stop Polish people from entering. The punks didn't succeed, however, and they gave up a short while later. The following year, the interior minister passed a law to stop Jews from slaughtering animals according to Jewish laws, but the law was soon abolished.[12] It was very difficult for Jews to get jobs as civil servants in the Polish government. Even so, although I heard rumors that a Jew couldn't become a general in the Polish army, we certainly had one prominent Jewish general – General Bernard Mond in Krakow.

Young Jewish and Polish men were both drafted into the Polish army at the age of twenty-one, but some Jews found ways to avoid military service. I even knew some who deliberately made themselves unfit for service by cutting a finger off their right hands or going on an extreme fast. Both Jews and Poles called these Jews "Moishe kara-binów" (Moses' rifles) after a line from a very funny popular song that poked fun at Jewish soldiers.

Of course, the Jews were not perfect. I know, for example, that some Jews bullied other Jews. In Krakow, for example, there were two brothers that were known as the "Jewish mafia." They were terrible people. They took protection money from poor vendors who could barely make a living. The vendors kept their meagre merchandise – shoelaces, little pocket mirrors, razor blades, shaving cream, shoe polish, buttons and so on – on a small table in a kind of open flea market called the Tandeta. One of the brothers came to the market-place every day to collect his "pay" from these poor Jewish vendors.

One day, this notorious gangster confronted a new Jewish vendor who had recently arrived from a small town and didn't know this man's reputation. It was the vendor's first day in this marketplace.

---

12 In order to ensure that meat is kosher according to Jewish law, it must be prepared by a *shoykhet* – a man conversant with the relevant religious teachings who is trained to slaughter animals painlessly and to check that the product meets the various criteria of kosher slaughter.

When the gangster asked the vendor for protection money, the vendor said to him in surprise, "I have no money and if I did, I wouldn't give it to you. Who are you to ask me for money? I have hardly enough money for bread!" The thug got very angry and kicked the vendor's small table into the mud and all his merchandise was ruined. The vendor was so upset that he grabbed a barber's razor blade from the mud and cut his attacker's throat.

The police arrested the vendor, for his own protection, and then called the gangster's brother and told him that if any harm came to the vendor, the police would hold him responsible and he would be charged. The surviving brother promised the police that he would give up his criminal business. All the newspaper headlines reported that the "terror of Krakow" had died a tragic death.

Although my father taught us never to start any fights, he also added, "If somebody hits you once, hit him back twice first and then ask questions." This advice served us very well and my father always supported us. We could defend ourselves with pride and dignity. No punk ever dared to come close to a member of our family. They all knew that we would take good care of anyone who hurt any of us.

I took boxing lessons at the Maccabi sports club in Krakow. I had a professional boxing trainer who was a sergeant in the Polish army. He was very good but tough. I quickly learned how to defend myself and how to deliver a strong punch to anybody who dared to attack me. I gained confidence in myself.

My father was very pleased that my younger brothers and I were well prepared to defend ourselves, but my dear mother wasn't too happy about it. Like any mother, she was afraid that we would get hurt. We assured her that we were only prepared to fight if any of us was in trouble. We were a strong, united and proud Jewish family, and we were respected by all our neighbours – Jewish and Polish.

One day, when Josel Meier was about six years old, he was playing with a Polish boy the same age and they got into a little fight. The father of the other boy came out of his house and pushed my younger brother to the ground. When my brother came home all dirty, my father asked him what had happened to him. Josel Meier described the event – that he had had a little fight with his friend and his friend's father had pushed him to the ground. My father went to the Polish man's house and asked him why he had pushed his son. The Polish man replied that he had seen my brother beating up his son. My father was so angry that he picked up the man and gave him a good beating, adding, "If something like this ever happens again, I will break you in half." I was standing right behind my father when he picked up a shovel and smashed the man's window, adding, "If you ever try to put your dirty hands on my son again, you'll be in much bigger trouble than you are now. This is only a warning." The Polish man took my father to court, and the outcome was that my father had to replace the broken window. I was very young but I remember being quite proud of my father for standing up for my brother.

~

I was a happy and active young man with a good social life in Krakow. I was a member of a Zionist youth organization called Akiva, a member of the Maccabi sports club for boxing and president of the Gwiazda (Star) sport club, which was part of the labour Zionist Poale Zion organization, where I boxed and played soccer and ping-pong. I had a lot of good friends at school, Akiva and the sporting organizations – Jewish and Polish. I also had a lovely girlfriend named Helen Shein, who was both gorgeous and smart. Helen had been brought up in a very religious home and we lived in the same building on Zamoyskiego 10. We loved each other very much and my family loved her too.

My friends and I had a lot of fun going to the park in the middle of Dietlowska Street or to Krzemionki, an archeological site and beautiful park with limestone rocks in the Podgórze district, or to the Vistula River to swim near the Wawel Palace. Although we didn't have cars, we managed to get around – we walked a lot and travelled by streetcar or horse-drawn buggy. Whenever we wanted to go out of town, we took buses and trains. Our family of nine didn't travel too much because it was expensive, but I had my own beautiful Kaminski bicycle. At the time, it was a luxury bike and I was very proud of it.

Of course, we didn't have television at the time, but in the evenings we read books and Polish and Jewish newspapers, and listened to the radio or to records played on the gramophone. On weekends, we had parties at home with our friends and family. I also used to go to a cabaret for a "five" – we said it in English – a social event for young people that went from five to eight o'clock in the evening. We got all dressed up and, for seventy-five groszy, we danced to a wonderful orchestra and got a cold soda and a piece of cake. We always had a really great time – to us the occasions were lovely and elegant and we enjoyed what we had. We cherished everything, especially our family and friends.

Our happiness, however, was overshadowed with dark clouds. On January 30, 1933, Adolf Hitler became the chancellor of Germany, the most powerful position in the German government. In March of that year, the German Reichstag (parliament) granted Hitler dictatorial powers and he ended German democracy. Using his special security forces – the Gestapo and the SS storm troopers – Hitler suspended individual freedom and suppressed all opposition.[13] He also began what would become his murderous campaign against the Jews.

The Nazis believed that the Germans were part of the "Aryan" race, which they considered to be superior to all others; they referred to themselves as the "master race."[14] They saw Jews and Gypsies (Roma

---

13 The Gestapo was the Secret State Police of Nazi Germany and the SS (Schutzstaffel) was a specialized police force that began as Hitler's elite corps of personal bodyguards. For more information on the Gestapo and the SS, see the glossary.

14 The word "Aryan" was originally a nineteenth-century anthropological term used to describe an Indo-European ethnic and linguistic grouping, and was changed by the Nazis to denote a Germanic "master race." For more information, see the glossary.

and Sinti) as a threat to the purity of the Aryan race, and the German people were brainwashed through an intensive propaganda campaign to believe in the Nazi doctrine. Their national anthem, known most commonly by its first line, "Deutschland über Alles" (Germany above All) reinforced the idea that Germany was above everything. Hitler quickly put in place policies that made life difficult for Jews in Germany. He soon also began planning the implementation of murderous policies against anyone who didn't fit his racial ideal. He had no respect for human beings. He was a threat to all Europe and a threat to all mankind.

Most people in Poland were really afraid of an aggressive Germany led by the monstrous Adolf Hitler. Although the Polish government assured us that we were safe, I didn't have much confidence in either the Polish government or the Polish army. I hoped that the world's leaders would wake up and stop Hitler before it was too late.

Poland entered into a defence pact with Britain and France in 1939; the two countries promised to defend our country if Nazi Germany attacked us.[15] Polish Marshal Edward Rydz-Śmigły, commander-in-chief of the Polish armed forces, said in a speech to all Polish citizens that he wasn't prepared to give up even one button from his uniform just because we had an agreement with the French and British governments. So it appeared that we now had a promise from France and Britain that they would come to our rescue, and we could also depend on our brave army. But we were still afraid of Hitler; we instinctively felt horrified and helpless. We saw a terrible future for us as Jews. I hoped that the world's leaders would be honest and stop the man we knew even then wanted to murder Jews, but they appeared to be indifferent to our plight.

---

15 For more information on the Polish-British Common Defence Pact (also called the Anglo French Assurance Pact), see the glossary.

Occupation and Loss

Before the outbreak of war, the Polish government had organized a defence force for Krakow. I was in a pre-military unit, so I was assigned to the defence of Krakow. I was ordered to join the fire department and had to go through six months of training as a firefighter. On September 1, 1939, when the German forces crossed the Polish border, I was at the Podgórze Fire Station and was assigned to duty on the tower.[1]

At four or five o'clock in the morning, I heard the noise of airplanes passing over the fire station. I pushed the alarm button and our commanding officer came up to the tower to see what was going on. When I told him about the noise, he told me that there wasn't any problem – the sound was coming from our own planes, called the Polskie Łosie (literally, Polish moose). A few minutes later, though, we heard the sound of bombs falling on the city. The German air attack didn't cause major damage to Krakow, although the train station suffered some damage.

I received an order from my superior officer to report to our head-

---

1 Germany invaded Poland on September 1, 1939, crossing into most major cities and swiftly taking control with aerial bombardments of Warsaw and with the use of firebombs in Krakow, Katowice and Tunel.

quarters. I had to go from Podgórze across the Piłsudskiego Bridge on the Vistula River and, as I approached the bridge, I saw, to my surprise, soldiers in different uniforms. Some people were screaming, "The English army is here!" while others were screaming, "The French army is here to help us fight the Nazis!" But when I got to the bridge, a Nazi soldier stopped me and ordered me, in German, to keep my hands up. It was terrifying. After about ten minutes, a German officer arrived on a motorcycle and asked me what army I was in. I told him, "I'm a firefighter for the city of Krakow." He asked me where I lived and when I told him that I lived across the bridge, he told me, as well as a Polish soldier standing guard on the bridge, to go home.

A few days later, the Polish government and the heads of the Polish military left Poland for Romania, leaving their citizens to the ruthless Nazi war machine.[2] I was on a fire truck headed for Romania as well, but I decided to jump off and go home to my family. The German forces quickly occupied all of Poland and panic broke out across the country. The Polish people – especially Jews – were terrified of the Nazis. We didn't know what was going on. We were frustrated, we were all alone and we were helpless. Our freedom was lost and our hardships began.

Soon the stores were emptied of basic foods and other articles. It became very hard to get milk, potatoes, bread, medicine and coal for the oven, so hunger became commonplace and our homes were cold. Most terrible of all, children went hungry and cried for bread, but their parents couldn't meet their needs. A black market developed for basic food, but the prices were so high that only wealthy people could afford to buy it. It became so difficult to get the things to survive that we all took for granted in normal times.

---

2   Polish government leaders, along with more than 100,000 Polish troops, escaped to neutral Romania on September 27, 1939. The Polish government-in-exile was formed first in France and then moved to London in June 1940 (after the fall of France).

In the years before the war, we had worried about the Nazis and especially about Hitler's hatred of Jews. But what the Nazi occupiers had in store for us was beyond our imagination. The Nazis came with the most modern weapons and used them against defenceless people. Under the direction of Governor General Hans Frank in Krakow, the Nazis ruthlessly terrorized, oppressed and humiliated the Jews.[3] To the Nazis, we weren't human beings. They seized Jewish businesses and stole our gold, silver, money, furs, radios, cameras, bikes, oil paintings – all our valuables. We were forbidden to work as doctors, architects, teachers, lawyers, rabbis and cantors. We were forbidden to go to public schools, high schools or universities. We were forbidden to go to public parks, beaches, cinemas, theatres, sport clubs, and Zionist and socialist organizations.[4]

After December 1939, we had to wear white armbands with a Star of David on them so the Nazis could identify us on the street, terrorize us and force us to work as slave labourers. As an added humiliation, we were forbidden to walk on the sidewalks. In Krakow, we were afraid to leave our homes because the Nazis hunted us like dogs on the streets and beat us up for no reason. They looked for Jews with beards, ordered them to put on their prayer shawls and then cut off their beards with their bayonets. It was painful for us to watch as the Nazis took pictures of their poor Jewish victims, asking, "Where is your God?" They also rounded up Jews and forced them to clean the sidewalks with toothbrushes. They knew how to degrade people, and they humiliated us daily.

The Nazis had established a Jewish council, or Judenrat, in

---

3 Hans Frank became governor general of the central territories of Poland, including Krakow, in late October 1939. This area, known as the *Generalgouvernement*, was a special administrative area specifically created to implement Nazi racial plans. For more information on the *Generalgouvernement* and Hans Frank, see the glossary.

4 These anti-Jewish laws came into effect in occupied Poland between October 1939 and February 1940.

Krakow on November 28, 1939, and its members worked hard to please the Nazis. The Jewish council had at its disposal a Jewish police force – the Ordnungsdienst (OD) – that was created in May 1940 with Symche Spira as its commandant.[5] Its officers wore uniforms with the yellow Star of David and Spira, dressed in a made-to-order uniform that looked like a general's uniform, had a lot of power over the Jewish population – especially later, when the Krakow ghetto was established in March 1941. He was sure that he and his men were very important, and he worked hard to be a good collaborator. Spira and his police forgot that they were Jews; they behaved like Nazis. The OD helped the Nazis terrorize our people.

I got enough abuse from the Nazis. I didn't need to be degraded and humiliated by Jewish police. In my opinion, they were Nazi police, not Jewish police. The Jewish police were no good to us at all.

The Jewish council also ordered the OD to pick up Jews to work as forced labour for the Nazis, and the OD carried out these terrible Nazi orders. People were taken from their homes or grabbed on the street; there was no place to hide. The work – cleaning toilets, offices, basements and streets – was intended to humiliate and degrade the Jews. They got no food and no money, only long hours and hard work. Sometimes, if a Nazi wasn't in a good mood or didn't like a Jewish worker, the Nazi killed him. Afterward he felt like a hero and didn't have to report the crime because the dead worker was only a "dirty Jew." These murders occurred at all times of day and night.

When the Nazi soldiers marched through the streets, the sound of their boots made our hearts beat faster. It was impossible to resist the SS, who were armed with machine guns and other weapons. We felt

---

5   The Germans established Jewish Councils (Judenräte) to administer the Jewish population and facilitate the implementation of their orders. In order to fulfill their role as community leaders and uphold order, the councils were assisted by the Ordnungsdienst, a Jewish police force. For more information on both Judenräte and the Ordnungsdienst, see the glossary.

so hopeless, unable to help one another, even our close families and friends. It was the beginning of the loss of our freedom, our culture, our pride and our dignity. Our only crime was that we were Jewish.

~

Toward the end of September 1939, my father and I heard that a bakery would be open on Kalwaryjska Street and that we could get one loaf of bread for our family. The only conditions were that we would have to pay a high price and we would have to go between six at night and six in the morning. So we lined up on the sidewalk in front of the bakery and around midnight, while we were still standing in the cold with other Jews and Poles, we suddenly saw all the Jews in the line run across the street – two Polish punks had ordered them to get out of the line. When these two punks came close to where my father and I were standing, they were surprised that we refused to obey their stupid order. We stood firm. The two punks tried to remove us by force, but my father and I gave them a good lesson. We gave them a beating and they gave up the fight.

Across the street, however, a German soldier stood on guard outside a building occupied by other German soldiers. He saw the commotion and called his superior officer, who came out with two soldiers. The officer took the two Poles and my father and me inside the building for questioning. Fortunately, the two Polish punks didn't speak German; they only pointed to us and said, "Jews." But my father was fluent in the German language – he had been a prisoner of war in Leipzig during World War I – and explained to the German officer that we had been standing in line for bread when the two young Polish punks started to act as if they were the law. My father told the officer that he understood that we all had to obey German laws.

The Nazi officer liked my father's explanation and asked the two Poles why they had behaved as if they were the law. He then ordered the German soldiers to give them a good beating. The officer told us that the two Poles would be sent to do hard labour in Germany to learn that they weren't Germans and shouldn't act like Germans. He took me and my father back to the lineup to get bread. All the Jews who had run from the lineup started to move quickly back into the line. My father and I became heroes – because we had stood firm, twenty or thirty Jews each had a chance to get a loaf of bread.

Around that same time, my father and I were walking in the Jewish Kazimierz district when we were stopped by a group of Nazi soldiers. They took us to a place not far away where about a hundred Jews were all lined up in a long column, four across. The commanding officer ordered all of us to hand over our money. Right in front of us, they shot three of the men standing in line, without any provocation. I was terrified and begged my father to give them our money. My father replied that the soldiers had killed the three men to terrorize us into giving them our money. He was right, but he could see how scared I was, so he handed over the five zlotys that we had. It was a real holdup – the Nazis behaved like bandits.

I was constantly trying to find food for our family, but one day in December 1939, while I was walking home from one of my searches through the deep snow, I was caught by the Nazis. I was pushed into a military truck that was loaded with other "Jewish slaves." We were taken to wash floors and toilets and to do other dirty, humiliating jobs in the Germans' accommodations, military barracks and offices, and private homes. I, of course, got no pay and no food but worked long, hard hours. As a "bonus" for our hard work, we got a beating. The work and beatings went on daily. I became more and more tired and hungry and I began to feel hopeless. I felt I had become a nobody with no hope for a better future.

As I would find out all too soon, the Nazis were beginning to send Jews to labour camps, where they forced us to do extremely hard, dirty jobs from early morning to late in the evening seven days a week.[6]

6   For information on the various kinds of Nazi camps, see the glossary.

In January 1940, I was again picked up on the street by the Nazis. Again, they pushed me and other Jewish victims into a military truck. When the truck was loaded up, it started to move. We stood pressed together, cold and hungry, and we had no idea where we were being taken. Our families didn't know where we were or whether we were safe or dead. The truck drove for hours – it was torture – and late that night we arrived at a large labour camp called Pustków-Dębica.[7] It was my first labour camp.

This camp was located in a large forest in deep snow. Our barracks was like a large warehouse, very dirty and unheated. Because our barracks was made of thin wood, the temperature inside was the same as the temperature outside: freezing cold. My sleeping place – the place where I was supposed to rest after a hard day's work – was a box of wood covered with thick ice. There was no mattress or blanket. The barracks floor was also covered with ice. The floor was like a skating rink.

I learned in this first camp that, as slave labourers, we would have to work in any weather – in rain, snow or frost. The camps were horrible, dirty places similar to large stables for animals. We got very little food. We had no choice but to work hard under the watch of the SS, who dressed in military uniforms, wore helmets on their heads and carried automatic guns. For our hard work we were paid with beatings by the SS or by the kapos.[8] We were stressed, tired and hungry. A lot of our people died from malnutrition, torture and executions.

At Pustków-Dębica, the Nazis ordered us to cut trees in the forest, in deep snow, and carry the logs on our shoulders to army trucks.

---

7 The city of Dębica, close to the village of Pustków, is about one hundred kilometres east of Krakow. The labour camp was originally created in 1940 to house prisoners assigned to build an SS training facility. For more information on Pustków-Dębica, see the glossary.

8 A kapo was a prisoner appointed by the SS to oversee other prisoners working as slave labourers.

The Nazis put together teams of two tall men and two short men, so the tall men in each team carried the whole load on their shoulders and the short men, who couldn't reach high enough, walked under the tree. The Nazis often beat us, having their fun while we worked hard. We had no winter clothing – no overcoats, gloves or sweaters – to protect us from the ugly frost and cold wind. A lot of us got frostbite – people lost their ears, their hands were crippled, and they couldn't move their fingers and feet. It was very painful to watch. Some of these people were sent home, but some were forced to continue working. We had no medicine or doctors or nurses to help us.

In the morning, we drank coffee that tasted like dishwater. In the evening, when we came back to our cold barracks, we ate old, stale bread and cold soup that looked like dirty brown water. Each portion of this so-called food wasn't enough for a small child, so we remained very hungry. We had no place to wash our hands. We had no toothbrushes, toothpaste, soap or towels. We had no change of clothing. We were dirty and we smelled bad.

When I had worked for the Nazis doing forced labour day and night in Krakow, I could at least go home to wash myself, have a little food and be with loved ones. In the labour camp in Pustków, however, I was far away from my family. I didn't know what was happening to them and they didn't know where I was or whether I was even alive. Living like this was devastating.

After a week of hunger, hard work, torture, bitter cold and Nazi terror, I decided to run away. It already felt as if I had been there for so much longer and it was impossible for me to stay – I knew that I couldn't survive that labour camp. Planning to escape from a camp well guarded by the SS and their well-trained dogs was dangerous – if anything went wrong, I'd be shot by the Nazi guards – but remaining in the camp was certain suicide. I had to take the chance. I asked my friend David, whom I had met in the camp, to escape with me and he agreed. We had to get through a strip of land about seven kilometres long between Pustków and Dębica. It was a risky idea, but it was our only chance.

A few days later, late in the afternoon, David and I started to move very slowly out of the camp. We faced numerous obstacles – barbed wire, patrols of Nazi guards with their vicious dogs, the bitter cold and the deep snow. We struggled through the deep snow for some time until we were freezing and tired. We could see a Nazi patrol with a dog in the distance. If the patrol spotted us, we would be shot on the spot. We dug into the deep snow so the patrol wouldn't see us, hoping that they would soon move on and disappear. We only had to hide in the snow for about twenty minutes, but it felt like hours. We were lucky, though; the Nazis didn't see us. Still, our strength was failing; we didn't know when we would be out of the danger zone and we weren't sure where we would be able to go.

Finally, late that evening, David and I came close to the town of Dębica. We looked for a safe place and some food, but it was difficult. The stores were closed and even if they had been open, we had no money and the stores didn't have much food anyway. Then I saw a house with a *mezuzah* on the door.[9] We knew it was a Jewish home, so we knocked and a lady came to the door. She saw two young Jewish men who were very tired, hungry and scared. This Jewish woman was a lifesaver. She made us a delicious hot meal – it was the best medicine we could have received. Her family asked us about the conditions in Pustków and we tried to describe them, but we were half-dead and wanted to go home to our families.

David and I waited in their home until it was late that night. The family gave us some money for the train to Krakow. We appreciated the great help that we got from them. We thanked them for their hospitality, said goodbye, and then we left for the train station. We had to watch out for the Nazis, so we were on guard all the time. It

---

9 A *mezuzah* is a small piece of parchment enclosed in a decorative casing and inscribed with specific Hebrew texts from the Torah. It is placed on the doorframes of the homes of observant Jews.

was illegal and risky for a Jew to travel by train or by other means of transportation, but we had no choice. We took the train to Krakow.

We arrived in the city after a scary night on the train. My family was very surprised to see me – they hadn't known what happened to me but had hoped that I was alive. The emotion at home was tremendous. We all cried out of happiness. For my family, my return to them was like a dream – it was a miracle that we were all together again.

I learned that my two younger brothers had also been in the same labour camp as me. They too had been caught on the street, pushed into a military truck and taken to Pustków. My brothers were also not dressed for the harsh winter and had suffered from the frost. After spending a terrible time there, they came home with frozen feet and ears. They had been released from camp because they couldn't work anymore – later on, people who couldn't work were killed. I couldn't believe that I hadn't seen Josel Meier and Abraham in Pustków!

I hoped that the Jews would get military help from the free world. We had young men and women who were able and willing to fight the Nazis. I was a young man who had military training, and I was not only able to fight the Nazis, I was also willing to fight and die, but with a gun in my hand. We wanted to get back our pride and dignity and defend our homes and families. But this was only a dream – the reality was that nobody in the world cared to help the Jews. We didn't get any leadership from Jews in the Zionist and socialist organizations either. We had had some strong Jewish leaders before the war, but since September 1939, both Jewish and Polish leadership had disappeared. Jews were left to the mercy of the Nazi criminals, who made our lives miserable with their barbaric behaviour.

I was soon picked up again – this time by the Wehrmacht, the German army, and sent to do forced labour every day in the buildings they had turned into army barracks. This time, though, I was lucky – I got to work in my trade as a house painter. I painted their premises and decorated and hung wallpaper. I worked there with a German soldier who was also a painter from Berlin. His name was also Willie and he spoke Polish quite well. After a few days of working with him, I asked him if I could bring my friend – a good painter named Jozef Szarp – to work with me. If Jozef could work with us, he could avoid doing dirty jobs for the SS. Willie told me to bring Jozef in the morning, so the next day Jozef appeared on the job.

When Jozef saw Willie – a German soldier – working alongside us, he got very excited and said to me in Polish, "Let's take that German animal to wash the toilets and floors and do all the other dirty jobs." I told my friend to shut up and I let him know that not only was Willie a very nice man, he also spoke fluent Polish. But Jozef ignored my warning and wouldn't stop making his stupid remarks. Willie heard everything, moved close to Jozef and said to him in Polish, "You are a little nothing. You have only a big mouth. You won't harm any German with your mouth – you'll harm only yourself. I would respect you if you came here with a machine gun and killed a few dozen Germans, but I don't respect your big mouth." Jozef was scared half to death; his face was as white as a sheet. Any other German would have killed him on the spot.

Willie used to go to all the soldiers in his barracks and collect cigarettes, bread and salami for me and the other painters. I taught him how to paint very thin lines on walls and he was grateful to me for that. After a day's work, Willie always had some food for the Jewish painters to take home. Whenever he came by with our food, Jozef stood aside because he was ashamed, but Willie always gave Jozef the same package that he gave the rest of us. The other German soldiers called him "Willie der Juden Freund" (friend of the Jews).

At the veterinary clinic for horses (*Pferde Krankenrevier*) in Krakow, another German soldier named Rudolf – also a painter – worked with us. Rudolf was about forty years old and not too smart, but we had no problems with him. After we'd had lunch with the German soldiers, Rudolf asked me, "How did you like your lunch?" When I said that I had enjoyed it, he told me that I had just eaten horse meat. He wanted to see my reaction, so I told him that I wished that I could take home some of that fine food to my family. The next day, Rudolf told me that we should be proud of our trade because the Führer, Adolf Hitler, was also a painter. I didn't know what to say. I couldn't tell if he was joking or serious, so I smiled and didn't say anything.

~

Shortly after the war began, the Soviet government opened its borders and many Jewish people tried to save themselves by crossing into the Soviet Union. But a lot of Jews didn't go. Some disliked the Communist regime and others didn't want to leave their homes and everything else behind. Older Jews, who remembered how well the German soldiers who occupied Poland in World War I had treated them, couldn't imagine the German evil that would emerge in World War II. And many Jews couldn't go to the Soviet Union because they had large families with small children. In our family, my mother was ill with arthritis and there were seven children, the youngest only five years old. It was impossible for all of us to go to the Soviet Union.

In early spring 1940, my good friends Leon Monderer and Jozef Szarp went to Lwów in Soviet-occupied Poland. They went through the open Soviet border and found freedom from Nazi oppression.[10] After they had found jobs in Lwów, they got a chance to come back to Krakow for a few days to see their families and friends. Before they left Krakow to return to the Soviet-occupied area, Leon and Jozef came to my house and asked me to go with them. They told me that they had a good job for me and that I should seize this opportunity to save myself from the Nazis. I had an impossibly painful decision to

---

10 Lwów, 350 kilometres from Krakow, had been annexed by the Soviet Union in September 1939 and more than 100,000 Jews fled there as refugees from the Nazi regime. On June 30, 1941, however, the German army took control of the region and the Jews living there were subjected to the same fate as those in the rest of Nazi-occupied Poland.

make. Should I leave my dear family in such a terrible time? I couldn't be of much help to them and I had the chance to be better off in Lwów with my friends. So I decided to be free and save myself. With pain in my heart, I decided to go.

My parents agreed with my decision; they wanted me to save myself from what was happening in Poland. My mother packed a suitcase for me with shirts, pants, socks and a jacket. I was ready to go. I said goodbye to my family and my parents pushed me to go with my friends, who were standing near the door. "I hope to see you soon," I said to them, but then looked back and saw my whole family holding onto one another. My younger sisters were crying. It was such a distressing image that I couldn't leave. I put down my suitcase and told my friends to go without me. "I hope someday we will see each other as free people," I said, "but I will not leave my family."

Leon and Jozef were sorry to hear my decision, but they understood my feelings. We all said goodbye and hoped to see one another after the war. It was difficult for me to say goodbye to my best friends because I couldn't shake the feeling that I would never see them again. But if I had gone with my friends, I would never have forgiven myself. I was so glad that I decided to stay with my family. I knew then that I could never leave my family behind and that I didn't care what happened as long as I was with my loved ones. It was the only way. I was only sorry that I couldn't be more helpful to them.

I still think about that time when I could have gone to the Soviet Union to save my life and escape the Germans. In Krakow, we were hunted by the Nazis as animals are hunted in the jungle. We suffered from hunger, terror and humiliation. It was exhausting to get through each day and it was unbearable to watch my family suffering. Not being able to help them made me feel helpless, angry and miserable. If only my family could have gone to the Soviet Union.

A few months after I resolved not to go to the Soviet Union, my father decided to move our family back to our birthplace of Wolbrom. Since it was a small town some distance from Krakow, we hoped that there would be fewer Nazis there and that our lives would be easier. We hired a Polish man with a large wagon and two horses to help us move. There wasn't much space in the wagon, so we could take only the most important of our belongings. We had no choice but to leave our furniture and oil paintings and the rest of our household goods behind in Krakow.

We travelled at night. Josel Meier and I went in the wagon with the Polish driver and the rest of the family went by train. It was illegal for Jews to travel by train, but we were desperate to get away from Krakow. On the road to Wolbrom I started to feel very dizzy and faint, so the Polish man stopped at a tavern and took me inside. He ordered a glass of hot vodka mixed with egg yolks and sugar and he told me to drink it all. After an hour, I felt much better. With the kind help of that Polish man, we arrived in Wolbrom late in the afternoon.

My father and I went to the Jewish council in Wolbrom to get a room for our family of nine. We had no place to go, so we had to wait out on the street. If a German patrol had seen us, we would have been killed on the spot or taken to a labour camp and probably ended up dying there. My father and I asked the president of the Jewish council, Splewinski, if he could give us a place or a room for our family, but he refused. He told my father that if I joined the Jewish police, then he would give us a room. We told Splewinski that we hadn't come for a job, just for a place to live. He repeated that he wouldn't give us a room unless we changed our minds. My father had known this rotten man since childhood, but it didn't make any difference – Splewinski refused to help us.

A Jewish man we called Kopel der Wasserträger (Kopel the water-carrier) was standing nearby, watching our exchange with Splewinski. As our terrible situation unfolded, he got very angry and offered to let our whole family stay in his room overnight. He was very poor and had one small room with a single bed and a small table but no chairs. We had only standing room all night, but Kopel went to sleep and left for work in the morning.

Kopel worked very hard for little money. He delivered pails of water to Jewish homes and also cut firewood for people in Wolbrom. He was an honest man with a good heart and we were extremely grateful to him. It had been a burden for him to have nine extra people in his small room, but he really saved us. We had expected a little help from the Jewish council in Wolbrom, but they weren't willing to help a Jewish family in danger. Instead, we got help from a poor, hardworking Jewish man.

In the morning, after Kopel had left for work, my father and I went to look for another place to stay. He knew some Polish people who lived in Wolbrom and took me to a building at number 4 Krzywa Street. When we went inside, a young lady met us and asked who we were looking for. My father replied that we were looking for a Mrs. Strzalka. The young lady introduced herself as Kazia Strzalka and said that Mrs. Strzalka – her mother – had died. Kazia said that she was now the head of the household and asked my father if she could be of any help. So my father told her that our family of nine was on the street and looking for a room. "Bring your family," Kazia said, "and I will try to get you something."

Kazia had a married sister, whose family name was Szafranski and who had two small children named Marylka and Ivonka. When the war broke out, the Szafranskis had moved into Kazia's building and had two large rooms. Kazia moved the whole Szafranski family into her apartment and we got their furnished apartment. Then our family was invited for a nice lunch. Kazia also had an older brother named Valerek who lived on the same floor and a sister named Balbina who lived in her apartment.

We were so fortunate to find such a decent Polish family during such terrible times. It was a real miracle. We were, after all, Jewish outcasts, but Kazia Strzalka cared about us and gave us shelter and moral support. Our apartment was right next to the Strzalkas' apartment – we lived there like one family and became very good friends. We felt a little better because of the Strzalkas and the Szafranskis, even though the Nazis in Wolbrom still posed a great danger to us. I will always be grateful to this fine Polish family.

In the winter of 1941, however, our situation drastically worsened. Lieutenant Eduard Baumgarten, a new and particularly brutal Nazi commandant of the gendarmerie – the Nazi paramilitary police force – arrived in Wolbrom to take charge of the town and the surrounding area. We soon got a sample of what to expect from this evil man. Shortly after he arrived, he killed eight Jews in one day to demonstrate his power. He was the law, the court and the police. He was a mass murderer, brutal, ruthless and cruel. He terrorized Wolbrom.

The day after this first atrocity, Baumgarten ordered the Jewish council to summon the best painting contractor to paint his living quarters, all his offices and the gendarmes' apartments. But when the Jewish council asked local painters to work for the commandant, they refused. One painter, Mr. Zarnowiecki, told Mr. Mager, the vice president of the Jewish council, that they didn't have to go to Baumgarten's office to be shot – they could stay at home for that. So Mager asked my father to take the painting job. I didn't like Mager and was ready to refuse the job because the Jewish council had refused to help us when we were on the street and in danger and had no place to go. But in the end, I felt that I had no choice but to work for Baumgarten. My father didn't like my decision, but he understood.

When Mager took me to Baumgarten's office, I have to admit that I was afraid. Baumgarten was a tall officer in a German police uniform. He had a stern face and didn't smile. He was a dedicated Nazi and I was going to have to work for him. He asked me, "Are you a good painter?" I said, "Yes, sir." Then he gave me a little speech. He said that he was expecting the best possible painting job and that if he wasn't happy with my work, I would be his ninth victim. What a pleasant place to work! Baumgarten told me to start painting the next morning. I knew my trade well – after all, I had spent three years training in a technical school for painters and I had lots of experience. But Baumgarten wasn't normal – he was a dangerous man and a monster. Just the sight of him terrified me. I hoped that I would find him in a good mood, that he would be pleased with my work and that I would be able to overcome my fear of him.

The next morning, I went to work for Commandant Baumgarten. The job was about one kilometre away from my home, on the outskirts of Wolbrom. I had no transportation, so I had to walk and carry my painting tools to the worksite. I didn't bring a lunch from home – we didn't have much food. The painting job wasn't too bad and I worked diligently so that I wouldn't end up being Baumgarten's ninth victim.

At lunchtime, Baumgarten came to see how the work was going. He was pleased with what I'd done, so he ordered me to go to the dining room to have lunch with his officers. I wasn't sure if I had heard him correctly, so I didn't go right away. A few minutes later, a gendarme came in and told me to follow him to a large dining room. I was put at a small table in the corner and given some very delicious food. I was uncomfortable, though – I wasn't sure about all this. I ate the same luxury food as the gendarmes, wishing that I could take some of that fine food home to my family.

After lunch, Baumgarten asked me if I could paint signs with decorations, German propaganda slogans in gothic lettering.[11] I said yes and asked if I could bring my two younger brothers to help me. He asked if they were skilled painters like me, and I said yes. In fact, as I've said, Josel Meier and Abraham weren't painters at all, but I knew that Abraham could paint professional signs, portraits and landscapes – Abraham was a genius; nothing was too hard for him. I felt that if Abraham were with us, I wouldn't be so afraid. I knew that the three of us could do the job and hoped that the evil man would

---

11 Gothic lettering is a style of handwriting that was used throughout Western Europe in the Middle Ages and continued to be used in German-speaking countries into the twentieth century.

like our work. Baumgarten agreed and the next day, Josel Meier and Abraham joined me.

We got a lot of work from Baumgarten, painting the offices and living quarters. We also painted Nazi slogans on the walls and gothic signs with Nazi propaganda. We worked under terrible stress. Baumgarten was satisfied with our work so far, but we were dealing with a monster, so we didn't know what would happen the next day. Even though our work was unpaid forced labour, knowing that Baumgarten liked our work gave me a little more confidence in myself.

One day, when I was working on a sign with gothic lettering, Baumgarten called me over and, to my surprise, told me that he was very pleased with our work and gave me some food to take home for my family. I didn't know what to think and was a little afraid. I couldn't believe that a murderer like him would give food to a Jewish family, but he appeared to be in a good mood. I thanked him, but said that I wouldn't be able to take it home because if a German officer caught me with the food, he would shoot me. So Baumgarten told me that when I left work he would assign a gendarme to take me home with the food. It was a miracle – our starving family actually got wonderful food from a Nazi murderer.

Baumgarten continued to behave decently toward me and my family and I still can't get over the fact that a mass murderer could show even a little humanity, if only to one Jewish family. I think that he was impressed with our painting and decorating, but that didn't alter the fact that he was still the terror of Wolbrom. On another day, I was working in a room when a gendarme shot himself in the room beside me. He couldn't take any more crazy orders from his sadistic boss. I knew that gendarme – he was a young German who used to watch me painting and spoke to me nicely. The incident was hushed up. Even Baumgarten's own officers were terrified of him.

As a painter for the gendarmerie, I also had to deal with Mager, the vice president of the Jewish council. On one occasion, when I went to buy paint at the paint store for Baumgarten, Mager was supposed to pay the Polish store owner for the paint. But Mager said derogatorily, "That Polack has a lot of money and I don't want to pay him." I was surprised to hear him say it and was ashamed of his behaviour. I apologized to the store owner, who told me not to feel bad. "It's a terrible war," he said, "so you'll always find injustice and terrible people." He could have made a lot of trouble for Mager and the Jewish council. All he would have had to do was report that he hadn't been paid for the paint and Mager would have paid with his stupid, arrogant life. When we made our next order, Mager had to go to the store by himself – I refused to go with him.

By April 1942 a portion of the town was sectioned off and became a ghetto, although a few Polish people still lived there as well. As bad as it was, at the end of that summer, everything suddenly changed for the worse: in early September, the Nazis ordered the deportation of all Jews from Wolbrom. We were ordered to take only what we could carry in our hands and given only thirty minutes to an hour to assemble in the market square. They gave us no time to think. The biggest tragedy of our lives had begun to unfold.

We were in shock. It was impossible to believe what was happening. I could see how horrified my parents and siblings were. We felt scared and paralyzed. We didn't know where we would end up or what would happen to us. There was nothing we could do to help one another. It was especially painful to see the confusion on the face of my youngest sister, Sarah, who was only ten years old.

We looked around our home for the last time and left. We knew that we would never come back. Then we ran to the market square in the middle of town. It was a very hot day. We assembled there in the terrible heat and waited for new orders from the Nazis. We had no water to drink and no food to eat. Thirsty and hungry children began to cry. In the past, the market square had been a community place where farmers came to sell their goods every Thursday. Now Jewish families were crowded together in the square, waiting to find out what the Nazis had in store for us.

Soon the market square became a place of terror. The Nazis and their collaborators – the Jewish police and the Ukrainian police – began to push and shove us.[12] We were beaten up for no reason. Then the Ukrainians began to kill a lot of our people by beating them with iron bars or shooting them. Adults and children cried for water to drink, but instead of getting water, they were shot.

I looked at my dear family with a broken heart because I couldn't help them. I felt especially powerless when I saw Sarah holding onto our mother for protection. She couldn't understand why we couldn't go home. Why were the soldiers killing our friends? Were we all going to be shot? She was scared – we all were scared and helpless in the face of this tyranny.

At this point, the Nazis ordered us to march more than one and a half kilometres to an open field on the outskirts of the town, near the railway station. We had to walk under the scorching sun – the heat was like fire coming from the sky. Our God seemed to have given us such a hot day so we could suffer even more. Our children were screaming and crying; they were scared, hungry and thirsty. The Nazis killed a lot of those children.

We waited for many hours in that field of barbarism. We didn't know what we were waiting for. We had no bathrooms, so we had to relieve ourselves where we were standing, among hundreds of people, including women and children. We were disgraced and ashamed. But the terror didn't stop – the Nazis and the Ukrainian guards continued killing Jewish men, women, children and babies. The blood of the murdered people was everywhere. It was devastating to watch our loved ones – especially our children – suffer so much and know that we couldn't help. Meanwhile, the Nazis walked around taking pictures.

---

12 The Ukrainische Hilfspolizei (Ukrainian Auxiliary Police) was formed in the wake of the German occupation of eastern Poland and the Ukraine in June 1941 and actively collaborated with the Nazis in the persecution, forced labour and mass murder of Jews. For more information, see the glossary.

Then, a few high-ranking officers – members of the SS who wore an insignia identifying them as medical doctors – came to this place of terror and started a deadly selection process. A Nazi doctor stood on a podium with a baton in his hand – like an orchestra bandleader – and directed his victims to the right and the left. Women and children were ordered to move to the right; men were ordered to the left. It soon became apparent from the selection that the children and older people would be murdered, while people able to work would live – at least for a short time, until they died of illness, overwork, hunger and torture. Hoping to be on the safe side, we ran in a panic from one place to another.

As the women were moved to one side, some of the Nazis pulled babies out of their mothers' arms. A lot of babies were murdered right in front of their helpless mothers. It was terrible to watch. Some of the mothers became numb and paralyzed; they couldn't move or talk. Mothers who tried to protect their babies were shot. Our people were dying by the minute; corpses lay strewn all over the ground like garbage.

A train pulling empty cattle cars arrived at the station and the Nazi murderers pushed our mothers, sisters, little brothers, babies and old people into the cattle cars. The cars were packed so tightly that people had no place to move or sit down; we knew that they had no food or water; there were no bathrooms. We were sure that the people inside couldn't get enough air to breathe and would suffocate. The Nazis pushed my mother and my four sisters into one of the cattle cars. My father, brothers and I all watched in horror but were helpless. It was the first time that I'd ever seen my dear father cry. Once a happy family man, energetic, a good provider for our family, my father was now a broken man. It was heart-wrenching to watch his suffering.

Inside the locked cattle cars, we heard people screaming and crying out. But after a while, we heard less and less crying. Our loved ones had no more strength to cry. Some were half dead; some had already died. Finally, there was only silence. After long hours of waiting in anguish, we watched the trains begin to slowly pull away. One of the guards told me that they were being taken to Treblinka.[13]

My father, my two brothers and I didn't know if we would ever see our dear mother and four sisters again. We didn't believe the story that they were being transported to a "labour camp" – the way that they were thrown into the cattle cars like trash and crushed inside them, we didn't believe that they could survive. I'm not sure how many of them were still alive when they arrived in Treblinka. It must have been so painful for my mother to see her four lovely young girls suffer on that train. How painful it must have been for all the Jewish mothers. To this day, it haunts me that I don't know if anybody survived that harrowing journey of death.

Then, my father, my brothers and I were pushed into another cattle car, which soon began to move. We too were pressed in like sardines in a can; there was no room at all to move. After spending many terrible hours in the cattle car, our train arrived in Krakow. Tired and hungry, we were pushed into military trucks and driven to the Krakow ghetto.[14]

The Krakow ghetto was yet another place of horror, an ugly, dirty place. During the month that we were there, we were terrorized by the Nazis and by many of the OD, the Jewish police. We had little food or medical help, so many people died from illness and starvation. There were so many corpses lying on the streets that nobody

---

13 On September 5, 1942, 6,000–7,000 Wolbrom Jews were deported to their death – most of them to the Belzec death camp, although some ended up in Treblinka. About 2,500 able-bodied Jews were sent to do forced labour. The Treblinka death camp was located about eighty kilometres northeast of Warsaw. For more information on Treblinka and Belzec, see the glossary.

14 The Krakow ghetto was established in March 1941 in the Podgórze district. More than 15,000 Jews were forced to live in a confined space that had previously housed only 3,000 people. When Willie Sterner arrived in September 1942, there were about 8,000 people living in the ghetto; the rest had been killed or deported to concentration camps.

paid any attention – we just walked over them. Our people died so fast that it was impossible to take care of them all. The burial squad was overworked, tired, hungry and stressed. We were homeless and dressed like beggars, wearing old, dirty, torn clothing, and most of us had no shoes. Little children had no shoes for their small feet and wore rags. Hungry, dirty and lonely, they asked passersby for food, but it was impossible to find a helping hand. There was so little food. Many of the children couldn't even walk anymore and lay on the sidewalks. It was heartbreaking.

We were the lost people. We were nobodies. We had so little strength that we felt we couldn't even think anymore; our minds felt shut down. We lived with indescribable brutality. We didn't know where our loved ones were. We were no longer a proud Jewish people.

Not long after we arrived in the Krakow ghetto, my father, brothers and I were forced into German military trucks, driven to the military offices of an SS unit in Krakow and put to work on road construction under inhumane conditions. Again, we received no food or money, only beatings. After long hours of hard work, the SS officers drove me and the others back to the ghetto. But no matter how tired and hungry we were, our most terrible pain was the memory of seeing our mother and sisters being pushed with such brutality into the cattle car outside Wolbrom.

The next day, the SS returned to the ghetto to pick up forced labourers for all kinds of jobs. They asked for a sign painter, so I volunteered. When they asked me if I was a good sign painter I said yes, which was a big mistake. I wasn't actually a very good sign painter – I knew something about it but I didn't have much experience. I used to help my father, who knew how to paint signs quite well. Nonetheless, I started working on a sign in an SS office.

After a short time, the SS-Hauptscharführer (master sergeant) who was in charge of the department came into my workplace to check my work. He came very close to me and asked, "Are you a sign painter?" With some chutzpah, which means nerve in Yiddish, I said yes. But when the SS man told me that his profession had been sign painting in Germany before the war, I knew that I was in big trouble. I knew that I might be shot or, if I was lucky, get fifty lashes. I was pretty sure that this would be the end of me.

To my surprise, however, the SS-Hauptscharführer didn't pull out his revolver and shoot me. Instead, he smiled and said that I was probably a good house painter. I told him that I was. I was very lucky – I think that what saved me was that he was a painter too. With even more chutzpah, I told him that I had a younger, more talented brother named Abraham who could make professional-looking signs and asked if I could bring him. The SS-Hauptscharführer said that it would be okay. Then I asked if I could also bring my younger brother Josel Meier and my father, who was a painting contractor in Krakow. The SS man said that when I was picked up the next morning in the ghetto, I should bring them all with me.

The next morning, the SS soldiers took us all to the SS-Hauptscharführer and he put us to work. My father, Josel Meier and I worked as house painters. We decorated and painted German propaganda slogans and symbols on the walls. Abraham painted signs with gold letters. We still worked under terrible stress, felt hungry and tired, but our situation was somewhat improved, if only temporarily.

Later, the SS-Hauptscharführer said that he was very pleased with Abraham's work and moved him into the office next to his and eventually made him the most important Jewish worker in the office. Abraham painted all kinds of propaganda signs and made blueprints. When I asked my brother how he was able to make blueprints, he answered, as usual, "Nothing to it. Anybody could make them." Even the SS respected Abraham's work.

A few days after we completed the work for the SS-Hauptscharführer, I managed to get a permit from him to go to Wolbrom by train to get some more clothing from the house we had lived in before the deportation. It was very unusual to be given this opportunity, but the SS officer got me the permit as a favour. Not that the permit would have protected me if I'd been caught – it was still highly illegal for a Jew to travel. At that point I had no intention of escaping the ghetto because, after all, my father and brothers were still there; all I intended to do was get some of our things to take back with me. But when I got to number 4 Krzywa Street, I found that the Nazis had sealed the door to our apartment. It was traumatic seeing this place again – all I could do was picture my poor mother's face and my four beautiful younger sisters.

Our former landlords, the Strzalkas and the Szafranskis, still lived next to our old apartment. I didn't have any place to stay, so Kazia Strzalka told me that I could stay with them. But at night, for my safety and theirs, I had to sleep in the barn with the pigs. It wasn't unusual for some people in the town to keep animals behind their houses and it was very dangerous to hide a Jew in a Polish home. If I were ever found there, I would be shot and the Strzalka and Szafranski families would be shot too. That was Nazi law. But they were willing to ignore the law and risk their lives to help me.

During the roughly two weeks that I was in Wolbrom, I learned that some Jews had been left behind to take care of all the Jewish households and valuables that remained after the deportation and the destruction of Wolbrom's Jewish community. The Jewish council, the OD and other Jewish forced labourers had sorted the valuables for the Nazis. There was no way for me to go into my former apartment to get clothing or anything else. There was nothing there.

Kazia Strzalka wanted to make Polish documents for me so that I could be a free man and "pass" as a Polish citizen. But whenever I thought about my own freedom and the suffering of my family, I got very confused and decided that I didn't want to have Polish documents. Instead, Kazia's brother, Valerek, who was an officer in the Polish partisans, registered me with his unit to fight the Nazis.[15] I decided I wouldn't go back to Krakow, but would try to fight instead.

---

15 Partisans are members of irregular military forces or resistance movements formed to oppose armies of occupation. For more information on the partisans in Poland during World War II, see the glossary.

Then, just as I was expecting to become a member of the Polish partisans, I heard some very tragic news.

In October 1942, SS thugs carried out an *Aktion* in the Krakow ghetto and murdered my father and two younger brothers.[16]

It was another terrible shock. In less than two months, I had lost my whole loving family – barbarically and for no reason at all. They were innocent victims. The Nazis took from me the most important part of my life. My heart was broken and my mind destroyed. The whole world seemed silent and indifferent. The injustice was almost too painful for me to bear. Now I knew that I was alone, left to suffer in this rotten world. I will always suffer the loss of my dear family.

We Jews hadn't declared war against anybody. Why were we so oppressed and so hated and so brutally murdered by the Nazis and their collaborators?

---

16 *Aktion* was the German word used to refer to a brutal roundup of Jews for forced labour, forcible resettlement into ghettos, mass murder by shooting or deportation to death camps.

Hard Labour

The murder of my father, mother, two younger brothers and four younger sisters by the Nazis shattered my whole life. I felt like I was in a coma. I couldn't think straight. I had a hard time sleeping because of nightmares. I no longer cared about myself or my future. I felt guilty for having left my father and brothers behind in Krakow and for hiding in the home of my best friends, putting them in terrible danger. Even though I somehow managed to find the strength to improve my situation at various times over the next three years of hell, the loss of my family often brought back these terrible feelings of helplessness and hopelessness.

I decided to leave my hiding place. I didn't tell the Strzalkas and the Szafranskis of my decision and didn't even say goodbye when I left their home because I knew that they would try to stop me. I was – and I still am – terribly sorry about not telling them what I was doing. I felt ashamed of what I was doing, but I wasn't in my right mind.

I was completely alone in the streets of Wolbrom and thinking about my family's tragedy when I was picked up by two Jewish police officers. They were there to liquidate all the valuables that had been left behind by all the Jews who had been deported. I had been a free man for only ten minutes.

I felt miserable. I was living my last minutes in Wolbrom, the small town where I was born, the last place where I had seen my dear family all together. Through all the terrible things that had happened since the war began, through all the hardships I had suffered, I had allowed myself to hope that some of my family would survive. Now, I took my last look at Wolbrom, where we had once been happy, and said goodbye forever. The moment was emotional and painful, but it was fleeting – I thought that my end would come soon and I didn't care.

The Jewish policemen pushed me into a military truck with other Jewish victims and we were taken to the neighbouring town of Miechów, about twenty kilometres from Wolbrom. The Nazis put us in a jail because, according to them, we Jews were the "criminals." The jail was dirty and smelled of urine. We were hungry but had no food or water. Inside the jail I met a friend of mine named Chaim Lokaj from Działoszyce, and we later met more Jewish victims from neighbouring towns such as Charsznica and Książ Wielki. We were there for many hours.

Finally, a military truck arrived and we were forced into it. The trip was hard on all of us. We were jammed very close together. We journeyed to a small labour camp near the Krakow airport and were put into large, dirty barracks.[1] There were more than a hundred people inside my barracks, so we didn't have much space to move around. We were all hungry, thirsty and tired. We were all despondent, all having lost loved ones in barbaric and evil ways. We were in terrible emotional pain. We didn't even talk to one another because all we could think about was our families, our friends and our sorrows.

During the couple of months that I was in the Krakow airport camp, I worked long hours on roads with a pick and shovel. It was dirty, brutal work. The weather was awful – cold rain mixed with snow – and I had no overcoat or gloves. I was afraid that I would get

---

1   The Krakow airport Willie Sterner is referring to is in Rakowice (northeast of Krakow) and was officially called the Krakow-Rakowice-Czyzyny Airport. The labour camp was known simply as Rakowice.

sick. The Ukrainian guards in their black uniforms watched us work. They weren't very friendly and made us feel even more miserable. We used to call them the "chubaricks" – I don't remember why, the word didn't have any special meaning.

There was another labour camp located near the airport and our camp – a *Landwirtschaft*, or agricultural camp where women prisoners did farming. This camp was a little better than most – at least the prisoners got more food – but it was still a Nazi camp and had vicious regulations. Working nearby, I saw a number of people I knew there – my cousin Sarah Horovitz, my friend Lola Olmer from Charsznica and my friends Fulek Brener and Berek Eisenstat from Miechów. It was good to see them, and I wished that I could see them more often.

One day, late in the afternoon, I was walking back to my barracks with my shovel in my hand after a hard day of work, hungry, cold and wet from the rain. Suddenly, I heard a loud voice calling my name. I was really surprised to hear my name called in this horrible place. I saw a Polish man walking toward me, and when he got closer I recognized him as Stefan, someone I had known in Wolbrom. He was working as a truck driver and was a free man, not a prisoner of the Nazis. I didn't know him well, but I was really glad to see him.

When Stefan saw how dirty and tired I was, he said, "Don't give up." He wanted to give me courage, to tell me that the terror would be over soon. When he saw that I was cold and wet, he gave me his overcoat. I felt a little warmer and thanked him for his generous help. Stefan replied, "I only wish that I could be of more help to you." He was going back home to Wolbrom for the weekend and said that he would see Kazia Strzalka. He knew that my family had lived in her apartment before the deportation in 1942. We talked a little while longer about our lives, about his family and about the terror. He was working for the Nazis and I told him to go back to work before he got into trouble. He smiled and answered, "We are in trouble even now." We said goodbye and shook hands, and then he went back to work. When he left, I felt alone and empty again. I never forgot this fine man and his friendship.

I didn't think too much about Stefan telling Kazia about my situation. How could Kazia help me when I was in a labour camp surrounded by barbed wire and guarded by Nazis with dogs? I didn't think that anybody could help me there – it was too dangerous to help a Jew. A few days later, however, I was called to report right away to the guardhouse located near the main entrance. I was scared about being called by the Nazis and set off with my heart pounding.

To my great and pleasant surprise, when I arrived at the guardhouse, I saw none other than Kazia Strzalka standing inside. She greeted me with a friendly smile. Now I was really afraid – not for me but for Kazia. When she saw the expression on my face, she told me in Polish, "Don't worry. It's okay." She had bribed the commandant of the guards – I can't believe that she had the chutzpah to bribe a Nazi – and had brought with her a suitcase full of warm clothing, warm underwear and gloves. She had also brought good food. Kazia said that Stefan had come to see her in Wolbrom and he had asked if she wanted to send me some warm clothing. He would be going back to his job at the Krakow airport and would be able to deliver the clothing to me in the camp. Kazia had thanked Stefan for his offer but said that she had decided to go herself the next week. She hadn't encountered any problems from the Nazis and told me in Polish that she would be back in about two weeks.

I was really happy to see Kazia, but I was worried about her taking such dangerous risks to bring me clothing and food. She had already risked her freedom and possibly even her young life by helping a Jew and bribing a German guard, which were crimes under German law. I was so grateful for her heroic help, but I told Kazia not to come anymore. It would be too dangerous for her to come again. But Kazia was determined to help me. She told me not to worry. And she did come to see me again with more winter clothing and food.[2]

---

2 On March 22, 1999, nominated by the author, Kazimiera (Kazia) Strzalka was recognized by Yad Vashem as a Righteous Among the Nations and her name was engraved on the wall in the Garden of the Righteous on the Mount of Remembrance.

~

I soon learned that there were painters who worked in their trade in the Krakow airport labour camp and that they lived in the barracks next door. I had known some of them in Krakow before the war, so after work one day I asked them if they could get me into the painters' unit. They promised me that I would be transferred into the painters' unit soon, but I waited for many days without getting any news, so I asked again. Again, they told me the same old story – I would be joining them soon. Meanwhile, I continued to work hard outside in the cold and rain mixed with snow.

By now I realized that my so-called friends weren't able or willing to help me get into the painters' unit. Maybe they didn't think it was important enough to risk asking the German boss for a job on my behalf. I was disappointed, but I didn't give up hope. Still nothing came my way and I soon got very discouraged. It appeared to be impossible to get a better job with the painters. I felt that nobody could change my terrible situation. I began to lose all hope.

At this low point, though, my luck changed. Some days later, the Nazi airport director – who was a very big fish – came to inspect the labour camp and the guardhouse. After the inspection, he went back to his office and I must have had either a lot of chutzpah or been very desperate because I followed him like a shadow as he walked past the guardhouse back to his office, just outside the camp. The Nazi guards didn't try to stop me – they were sure that I had been asked to accompany the director. The whole time that I walked behind him, he never looked back. After about ten minutes, I started to talk to the director – I was afraid because I had left the camp illegally – and told him that I was an excellent house painter. He didn't say anything. He didn't even turn his head toward me.

When the director went into his office, I followed him. He sat down at his large desk and started to write something. I kept telling him that I was a professional house painter and that I would like to work in my trade. Suddenly, the director stood up and said, "We have many so-called good tradesmen – painters, carpenters, electricians and others – but they don't even know how to start a job." I overcame my surprise that he had talked to me at all and said that if I turned out not to be a good painter, he could always shoot me (as if he needed my permission). I was that desperate. The director didn't say anything and walked out of his office. I waited for about ten minutes, but he never came back. I wanted him to come back because I now had a really big problem – with my Star of David armband I was obviously a prisoner outside the camp fence but I was still surrounded by Nazi guards. If the guards thought that I was trying to escape they would shoot me on the spot, so I had to figure out some way to get past them and back into the camp. I started walking toward the guardhouse and, as I approached the guards, I just kept walking, trying to look as though I had permission to be where I was. Luckily it worked. The guards didn't try to stop me because they assumed that I had been doing some work for the director.

In the evening a few days later, after I had finished a hard day of work in the rain and wind, when I was feeling especially miserable, hungry and tired, the door to our barracks opened and in walked a friendly gentleman named Max Shnitzer. He was in charge of the painters in the barracks next door and was there to give me good news: the next morning I would go to work in my trade. I had to report to the painters' kapo who would tell me where I would go to work. Shnitzer wished me good night and good luck in my new job and left. I was shocked, surprised and nervous, but also very pleased. The opportunity to change from doing miserable hard labour to working as a painter was a big deal for me. I was sure that I would be much better off because I was skilled at my trade and I would be able to work inside. But then I remembered that I had told the director that he could shoot me if I wasn't a good painter – that hadn't been a very smart idea, but the damage was done.

Overall, I had high hopes for my new position, but my situation was still precarious. What kind of Nazi monster might my new boss be? How would he react to me? Would he make my life even more miserable than it was now? All I could do was hope that things would work out for the best.

Early the next morning, all the painters assembled in front of the barracks. The Nazi guards put us into a military truck and drove us to Karmelicka Street in Krakow. Our guards were black-uniformed Ukrainians and the SS. I met some painters I had known from better times in Krakow before the war, and two of them had attended the same technical school for painters as me. They were glad that I had made it into the painters' unit and that I would be working with them. They hoped that I would be okay and said that I shouldn't worry about the director.

Our boss was a Nazi, a civilian now living in Krakow, who was in charge of the painting department for the largest painting company in all of Europe, Birkle and Tomas of Germany. He said to me, "You're supposed to be a capable painter." I told him that I knew my trade well, that I hoped he would be pleased with my work and that I would try my best. But I never knew what to expect from the Nazi sadists. They weren't normal. They specialized in evil, in committing heinous crimes and atrocities.

My boss put me into a large room and told me that I had to paint the whole room – the walls and the ceiling – and be finished by four o'clock that afternoon. Then he left the room without giving me any instructions. He didn't tell me where the painting tools were or where I was to get the paint. I knew my trade well, but even I needed to be told what had to be done and in what colours. So I hoped that the Nazi boss would come back soon to tell me what to do. I waited and waited but eventually realized that he wouldn't come back until four o'clock.

I started to panic. I was an excellent painter, but I didn't know where and how to start the job, and I had only seven hours to finish it. I knew that a Nazi wouldn't accept excuses – if I didn't finish the work in time, I was sure to be tortured, beaten or shot. That was how the Nazis worked. Now I regretted that I had managed to get into the painters' unit. I felt as if I was stuck in the middle of the ocean, powerless to save myself.

I started to look for a clue as to how to start the job. I looked over at the long table and saw a brush with short bristles that was almost square-shaped. I had never seen a brush like it. Although I had worked for my father's painting company and had seen painters' supplies from the Wolfrum company of Vienna, had worked for painting contractors in other Polish cities and had finished three years of the technical school for painters in Krakow, I had never seen a square-shaped brush – 13 centimetres by 12 centimetres – with a handle. On the floor near the table, I found a large barrel with clear liquid, a large box of sawdust and a few rags. I couldn't give up now.

I put my hand into the liquid. It was odourless and colourless, but it was sticky. I wanted to clean my hand, so I put it into the sawdust, but the liquid didn't come off so easily. The clock was ticking and I was still in a panic, but I began to think – was a combination of the sawdust and the liquid the solution to my problem? I took a piece of wood from the floor and covered it with a mixture of liquid and sawdust. It looked ugly, but when I punched the ugly patch with the funny square brush, to my surprise it became a nice design. At least it looked nice to me, but who knew whether my Nazi boss would like it?

The clock was ticking, so I decided to work with the liquid, the sawdust and the square brush. My painting experience and schooling were a great help to me, but I also needed luck because this job wasn't typical for an ordinary painter from Poland. The work looked beautiful to me – it was a brown-coloured natural crocodile design – and I did finish on time.

At about four o'clock in the afternoon, my boss came into the large room and looked over the job. My heart was pounding as I waited for his verdict. He turned to me and smiled. I wasn't sure about his smile – Nazis had also been known to smile when they killed people – but he said that he had been sure that I wouldn't be able to finish the job.

This painting material was a new product from Germany, he told me, and only a few German contractors had begun working with it on a trial basis. Still smiling, my boss told me that I must be a very smart painter because I had figured out how to do the job with new tools, no regular paint and no supervision. He was pleased with my work and he assured me that the airport director would not shoot me. Then he left the room.

I was extremely relieved – this had truly been a matter of life and death.

My boss came back with food and cigarettes for me. I ate and felt as satisfied as I did after breaking the fast at Yom Kippur.[3] I even had some food to share with my close friends. It wasn't much, but it gave us some respite from our daily hunger.

After that experience I wasn't as afraid and worked with more confidence. My Nazi boss had more respect for me – he even came to ask for my opinion about painting and we made decisions together about painting jobs. I was very surprised when he told me that if there wasn't a war on he would take me to Germany to work at Birkle and Tomas, where he was a big wheel. He said that I would have had a very good future with them. It was nice to hear such things, especially from a Nazi – most of the time I was humiliated or beaten by them.

In June 1942, the Nazis established a *Zwangsarbeitslager* (forced labour camp) in Płaszów, a suburb of Krakow, and that winter all the Jewish prisoners in the camp at the Krakow airport – including me – were moved there.[4] The new camp had about 20,000 prisoners,

---

3 Yom Kippur, the Day of Atonement, is a solemn day of fasting and repentance. For more information, see the glossary.

4 The camp in Płaszów was built on the grounds of two former Jewish cemeteries and operated solely as a labour camp until January 1944, when it was converted into a death camp. At its height, the camp held about 20,000 inmates, including hundreds of prisoners from the Warsaw Ghetto Uprising that took place between August and October 1944.

including Poles, Germans and Gypsies, but the majority of prisoners were Jews. The camp commandant was Oberscharführer Zdrojewski and although he was easygoing compared to some of the other SS men I had experienced until then, the camp conditions were horrific. We lived in large stables like animals, with no hygienic facilities – no place to shower, not much water, no toothbrushes or toothpaste, no towels and no soap. We had no change of underwear or socks. We only had torn, old clothes that we wore at work during the day and at night when we slept. We were dirty and covered with lice – another enemy for all of us. We were hungry all the time. We were on a very strict food regimen – what we had of it, though, could barely be called food – maybe it was fine for pigs, although I doubted that even pigs would like it.[5] Once, we were given some food named sago and even though I was very hungry, I couldn't touch it because it smelled like dead fish.[6] But some of our people were so starved that they couldn't let it go to waste.

At six o'clock every morning, in rain or snow or frost, we had to run out of the barracks for *Appell* (roll call), where we were all counted. Then, after drinking dishwater coffee and eating a mouthful of old bread, we worked long hours, seven days a week. We had to endure regular beatings for no reason by the Nazis and the kapos. We were always exhausted and felt half-dead. If we got sick, there were no doctors, dentists, nurses or medicine. We were constantly degraded and humiliated.

The commandant of the Jewish police force in Płaszów was a man named Wilek Chilowicz. He and his wife, Marisia, wore fancy uni-

---

5   The daily food ration for each prisoner at Płaszów was 200 grams of bread, 150 grams of cheese, 300 grams of coffee substitute and hot water soup; occasionally one egg was added.

6   Sago is a starchy foodstuff, similar to tapioca, which is derived from the soft inside trunk of various palm trees; it is mainly used in making puddings and as a food thickener.

forms with the Star of David that looked as if they had been tailored for a general. Chilowicz and Marisia took orders from the Nazis to make our lives more miserable, but they also made decisions on their own. I had known Marisia Chilowicz well in Krakow before the war, although her name then was Jakubowicz. She was my next-door neighbour in Podgórze – I lived at Kalwaryjska 25 and Marisia lived at Kalwaryjska 23. I knew her family well too, and I sometimes used to go to their home. Her parents were lovely people and Marisia was a nice Jewish girl. We were good friends, and Marisia and I even went to dances at the Dom Akademicki (student residence) on Starowiślna Street together. But in Płaszów, Marisia Chilowicz was terrible. She was under the impression that she was better than us, the rest of the Jewish prisoners.

Once, Marisia stood on a podium in front of thousands of Jewish victims – men and women, young and old – in the Płaszów camp and gave a vulgar speech to all of us. She humiliated and degraded us, especially the women. Most of us were shocked to hear such a speech from a young Jewish woman; we all had red faces. If I hadn't been there myself I wouldn't have believed that Marisia was able to give such a vulgar speech. How could a nice, young Jewish woman like her change into a monster, a Nazi helper? It was hard for me to understand. I think the Nazis must have destroyed her mind; they had so many ways to destroy our people.

At Płaszów, I was back to working long, hard hours, breaking stones with a small hammer outside under terrible conditions. But a few weeks later, I was ordered to work as a painter in the paint shop. We did small jobs around the camp. When a transport brought men and women to the camp, we had to paint yellow stripes on their clothing to humiliate them. Later, we got a new foreman named Mr. Greenberg, an older Jewish man I had known before the war. He was a painting contractor in Krakow and a fine gentleman.

In February 1943, we got a new camp commandant, a notorious

SS captain named Amon Göth who was known for his brutality.[7] His first action at Płaszów was to order the construction of a gallows. Göth then hanged eight Jewish men just to assert his power and authority. He had a large, vicious dog named Ralf. Göth quickly achieved his evil goal – we were all afraid of him. We even feared his name.

Not long after his arrival, Göth decided to paint his cottage, so he ordered my foreman, Greenberg, to come to his cottage and do the job, but Greenberg wouldn't go by himself. He told me that I had to go with him, so we went to the cottage to meet the terrifying commandant. Göth was waiting for us with his dog. He was a tall, mean-looking man and he greeted us with an ironic smile on his face. He told Greenberg that he wanted us to paint both the interior and exterior of his cottage with the best paint. He wanted the finest workmanship, wanted the job finished within forty-eight hours, and the only pay would be terror. Greenberg responded to his ordering by simply saying, "Yes, sir." Then, pointing to the gallows, Göth told Greenberg that if the job wasn't finished to his satisfaction in forty-eight hours, all the painters would hang.

Greenberg was terrified – he was shaking and trembling. All the other painters were also scared. We were well aware that Göth was prepared to keep his promise, that he would be only too happy to hang us all if the job wasn't finished on time.

After Göth left with his dog, I asked Greenberg, "How do you expect to finish this painting job in forty-eight hours? With whom, and with what tools and materials?" I was the only able painter in our paint shop. Mr. Greenberg was too old for this work and the others in our shop were two musicians, brothers Henry and Poldek Rosner. They didn't know how to paint. Their main job was to serenade Göth

---

7   For more information on Amon Göth, see the glossary.

after he had finished a day of killing innocent victims. The Rosner brothers had been assigned to our paint shop *not* to paint. How were we going to do the job?

I asked Greenberg why he hadn't told Commandant Göth that we didn't have the tools and materials or even the manpower to paint his cottage. Göth would have shot him if he had complained, Greenberg whimpered. "Now," I responded, "Göth will hang all the painters." Greenberg was afraid to go to Göth's office to raise our concerns, but he was also afraid that all the painters would hang because of him. He asked me to go with him to Göth's office to explain our problem. It was a huge risk because we had no guarantee that Göth wouldn't shoot us just for having the nerve to go to his office, but we had no choice, so we went.

My heart started to beat faster when we got to the office. An SS guard let us in when we explained why we were there. Göth looked at Greenberg and me, and then asked Greenberg what he wanted. But even though Greenberg was fluent in German, he couldn't speak because he was so terrified of Göth. I could see the end of us right there. Göth stood up and started to scream at both of us. Greenberg tried to talk but couldn't form any sentences. So Göth turned to me and asked why we had come. I told him that we weren't equipped to paint his cottage. I told him that we were willing to paint it, but we didn't have the paint, tools or painters to do the job in forty-eight hours.

To my surprise, Göth spoke to me calmly. He asked what could be done and I told him that if we could go to the Krakow ghetto, we could get all the materials and tools we needed, as well as some good tradesmen. He agreed. He gave us an SS man with a military truck and we went to the ghetto, where we had no problem finding our lifesaving paint, tools and painters. Then we had to return to our hell in *Zwangsarbeitslager* Płaszów.

We now had all that we needed to start the painting job, but we still had to please Göth, the sadist, executioner and angel of death. If we didn't, we all would go to the gallows. Any Jewish prisoner who had to work for Göth was terrified until Göth accepted the finished job. He was only too happy to kill Jews. He didn't need any reason to kill – to him, we were objects for target practice.

I had hoped that my foreman, Greenberg, would organize the work to finish in time, but he put me in charge and told me to prepare and organize the whole job – he was so scared that he couldn't function. He was afraid that he would make a mistake that would cost us our lives. I had no choice but to take on that horrifying responsibility. Greenberg was very relieved that I agreed to take charge of the painting job and the lives of the Jewish painters, but I wasn't too happy about it.

I started by putting about ten women to work washing and cleaning the floors and the woodwork and then put some of the painters to work with a spray gun and lime paint for the ceilings and walls. I put some of the other painters to work with oil paint on the newly washed woodwork. The women also washed and cleaned after the spray work was done. I was very lucky – I had ended up with a good team and good cooperation, but we worked nonstop for forty-eight hours. We were all hungry, so I went to the camp kitchen and asked the cook, a German Jew named Meyer, whom I knew well, to provide food for my hard-working people. At first Meyer said that he would help with coffee, but when I persisted and asked him to give us some bread as well, he said okay. I was very happy when he managed to give us soup and bread. The food was a great help, especially when we were working under such terrible stress, without any sleep for forty-eight hours.

We did finish the job in time. We gave Commandant Göth a professional paint job with the best workmanship. But we were still nervous. Perhaps he wouldn't be pleased with our work. Who knew how Göth would react? Soon Göth arrived with his dog, Ralf, and we all awaited his verdict. To our huge relief, Göth told Greenberg that the job had been done well and on time, so the foreman could come to his office to pick up some cigarettes for the painters. Greenberg said that he would come and Göth left with his dog. We were glad that

Göth was pleased with our work, but we couldn't understand why the commandant had offered us a bonus.

I asked Greenberg when he was planning to go to Göth's office to pick up the cigarettes and Greenberg replied that he had no intention of going – he was just happy that our big problem with Göth was over. Then I made a stupid remark. I said that if he didn't go to Göth's office for the cigarettes, Göth would think that he was ignoring his offer. Greenberg looked at me and said in a frightened voice, "You're right. I have to go." Then I was sorry for my thoughtless comment. I was sure that Göth wouldn't remember his promise and I would be responsible for anything that might happen to Greenberg.

Greenberg asked me to come with him. It was dangerous to go, but I didn't think that I could refuse. Terrified, Greenberg and I walked to the office of Commandant Amon Göth to pick up the cigarettes. To our surprise, however, Göth gave us enough cigarettes for all the painters – a real luxury item in *Zwangsarbeitslager* Płaszów. Thankfully our painting job was finished and I hoped that we wouldn't have any more problems with Göth over the work.

But I saw a black future for all of us. *Zwangsarbeitslager* Płaszów was a big, open jungle – Göth and his gang were the terrible hunters and we were the animals. Göth's favourite pastime was shooting unarmed, helpless victims. His biggest thrill was mass murder. He killed people whose faces he didn't like. Wherever he went, people died. We were easy targets for the Nazis – we had no place to hide. They couldn't miss. We didn't fight back because we had no strength left and couldn't function properly. We couldn't get close to the Nazis or get any weapons. The camp was a human slaughterhouse. New transports of Jewish prisoners constantly arrived from smaller towns and villages. It seemed that as soon as a hundred Jews were slaughtered in Płaszów, a hundred new Jewish prisoners arrived to replace them.

And in the evening, after a day of hunting and shooting innocent men and women, Göth would call his musicians, Henry and Poldek Rosner, to play soft music for him while he and his company drank fine wine and enjoyed themselves.

One day, Commandant Göth came into the paint shop where I worked for a special inspection. We still had only four official painters in the paint shop and I was the only real painter. We worked on small jobs around the camp. But when Göth came into our paint shop, he was surprised to see thirty to thirty-five men. They were all new arrivals from the Krakow ghetto and had been placed in the paint shop until other jobs could be assigned to them.[8] Göth called for the foreman, but Greenberg wasn't there at the time, so another man stepped forward and said that he was the foreman. He was a painter who had just come from the Krakow ghetto and he had been waiting in the shop for a job. Greenberg had actually gone to try to find work for him and the others. I had known this self-appointed foreman before the war. He made a big mistake when he said that he was the foreman.

Commandant Göth looked at the "foreman" and asked how many men were in the paint shop. He replied that he wasn't sure. Göth asked what kind of work was available for everyone and again the "foreman" said he wasn't sure – he thought that the painters were painting red stripes on pails for the fire department. Then Göth asked how many pails he had. The self-appointed foreman said that he had about fifty pails. When Göth asked how long it took to paint one pail, he couldn't answer.

At this point, Göth ordered one of the painters to paint a red stripe on one pail. The job normally took about five minutes, but in the presence of Göth it took only two minutes. Göth started to go crazy. He took out his revolver and, in front of all the other painters, shot the man from Krakow who had claimed to be the foreman. In the second row of painters, the victim's father watched the murder of his son. The poor man fell down on his knees in shock. Luckily, the

---

8 On March 13, 1943, during the two-day process of liquidating the Krakow ghetto, about 6,000 residents were deported to the forced labour camp at Płaszów.

men next to him grabbed him and kept him on his feet. If they hadn't helped him, the father would have been shot just like his son. We all watched the terrible drama unfold, paralyzed and unable to help.

Running like a mad dog from one place to another, Amon Göth decided that every second painter would be shot. We were all terrified. I was standing next to Poldek Rosner in the lineup. I asked him to explain to Göth that there had been a misunderstanding and that we weren't at fault. Poldek Rosner stepped out of the lineup and asked Göth for permission to speak. Wearing his ironic smile, Göth asked Rosner, "What is it? Do you have something important to tell me?" Rosner began to explain about the new men having just arrived from the Krakow ghetto and having been placed in the paint shop until they were given jobs. Our foreman, Greenberg, had gone to find work for them.

When he heard this, Göth got very angry. Screaming, he demanded to know why he hadn't been told what was going on. What a joke! As if Göth had ever regretted murdering an innocent man for no reason – he was never sorry for killing anyone. But when he heard Rosner's explanation, Göth changed his order. Instead of having every second man shot, he ordered a new penalty of twenty-five lashes for every new painter. Old painters would get only five lashes.

After this incident, I continued working in my trade as a painter, but the work got harder every day and I fell into a kind of depression. All I could think about was my loving family being brutally ripped away from me by the Nazis. The pain of that picture stayed with me constantly. I tried to be optimistic, but it was impossible, especially when I saw what was going on around me. I saw that our lives weren't worth one penny. I saw the SS men shooting and hanging our people and the Nazis looking for more victims to murder. It was even dangerous to go from one barracks to another when working in the camp. If a Nazi wanted to have fun while I was walking to work by myself, he could easily shoot me. It was clear that the other Jewish prisoners and I would eventually but surely be murdered. There was no escape.

In late March 1943, at a hill close to Płaszów called Chujowa Górka, bulldozers dug a mass grave to hold some of the victims from the final liquidation of the Krakow ghetto. The digging of the grave was a big production. When it was ready, some of the victims were shot on the hill and pushed down into the pit by bulldozer. Some of them were already dead when they fell in, but others were only wounded and died horribly in this mass grave.

Life in Płaszów was unbearable. I was desperate for a change, so when a request came into the Płaszów office from the Skarżysko-Kamienna labour camp for a specialist painter, I volunteered for the job.[9] I was the only one there who could do the job – the camp authorities in Skarżysko wanted someone who could not only paint signs but also had knowledge of decorative painting and paper hanging. I knew that Skarżysko was a bad camp, but it wasn't as if I was expecting to end up somewhere that was better.

Foreman Greenberg, however, told me that I couldn't go to Skarżysko. He argued that I would just be exchanging the bad for the worse. I asked him, "Is there any place worse than here?" He replied, "Yes. All the concentration camps are very bad for Jews, so don't look for another problem. Here you know the terrible things we all have." I saw that he was right, but I also felt that perhaps a move to another place would at least improve my morale. I needed to find some way to stop feeling so hopeless. The truth is, though, that there wasn't anything that could accomplish this – I was a Jew in Nazi-occupied Poland.

In the end, Greenberg did manage to stop me from going to Skarżysko. He told me that whenever a better job came up for a paint-

---

9 The forced labour camp in Skarżysko-Kamienna, a town in east-central Poland, was established in 1942, after the town's entire Jewish population was deported to the Treblinka death camp. Between October 1942 and August 1, 1944, when the camp was liquidated, 25,000–30,000 Jews were brought to Skarżysko-Kamienna; 18,000–23,000 of them died there.

er like me, he would send me. Greenberg liked me a lot – he was like a father to me, watching over me and helping me any way he could. So I stayed in Płaszów. There was no change for the better – only more hardship and killings and suffering.

In the spring of 1943, Greenberg came to me with a smile on his face. He told me that he had received an order from the camp office for a specialist painter who could retouch old damaged oil paintings, paint signs and decorate enamel cups and plates as gifts for high-ranking officers. I was the only one available for the job. Greenberg asked if I remembered how he had refused to let me go to Skarżysko and his promise to send me to a good job if one came along. He said that I was now going to a new place, a better place. I was going to Oskar Schindler at the Deutsche Emailwaren Fabrik (DEF) at 4 Lipowa Street in the Zabłocie district of Krakow.

Oskar Schindler

I had never heard of Oskar Schindler or the Deutsche Emailwaren Fabrik, but I was happy to leave Płaszów.[1] I thanked my friend Greenberg for keeping his promise and said goodbye. Greenberg said that he wished he could go with me because he had heard that things were very different at Schindler's place. I was ready to see what was different and hoped that Greenberg was right.

A guard took me to the Emalia, the enamel factory. A guardhouse stood on the left side of the front entrance. I gave my papers to the guard and he took me to the office on the right side of the entrance. My heart was beating furiously – who knew what would happen in this new place? I was greeted by Schindler's secretary, a lovely young Polish woman who smiled at me – that was a pleasant surprise – and said that I was all registered to start work. She said that I would be fine there, that I shouldn't be scared, that I was in a good place. Then she wished me good luck.

My new camp was at the back of the enamel factory. Compared to Płaszów, the camp was small. The barracks were much smaller and

---

1 Oskar Schindler's enamel factory was located close to Płaszów but instead of transporting workers back and forth from the labour camp, Schindler had, at his own expense, built a subcamp with barracks on the site. Although Willie Sterner did not know it yet, this was one of several ways that Schindler tried to protect his workers.

there weren't as many barracks nor as many inmates in them. The camp looked a little better than Płaszów, but it was still a labour camp officially under the command of Amon Göth.

I asked a Jewish man who worked there if conditions in this camp were the same as in Płaszów and he said that they weren't, that I would be safe because of the fine director Oskar Schindler. We were much better off than people in all the other camps, he told me, even if we were affiliated with Płaszów. We were very lucky to be here because we were being watched over by an angel. I felt a little better after talking to him and hoped that it would turn out to be true.

The next morning, I was called to Oskar Schindler's office. He was a tall man with a friendly smile and he greeted me warmly. I was surprised that a German industrialist would talk to me not as a Jew but as a normal person. When he asked for my name, and I told him that it was Willie Sterner, he said that he would call me Willie. He talked to me the way a proper boss talks to a worker. I immediately felt more relaxed and comfortable with him. I wasn't afraid of him. I thought that I must have been having a nice dream because I knew that Schindler was a member of the Nazi party, and I didn't expect decent treatment from a Nazi.

Schindler asked me if I knew how to retouch old, damaged oil paintings. I said yes, that I had done that kind of work in Krakow. At the technical school for painters, I had helped my art teacher Professor Wagner retouch oil paintings at the Wawel Palace. I had also refinished antique furniture, so I said yes with confidence. Smiling, Schindler said that I would work out well there.

I needed tools, tubes of oil paint, and some dryer and turpentine, so Schindler drove me in his fancy car to buy the materials for my work. I was a free man for a few hours. Even though, when we got back to the Emalia, I lost my freedom again, my good friend Greenberg had been right – Schindler's camp was a much better place. I was very grateful to Greenberg and wished that he could come too.

I met other Jews at the Emalia – about 1,000 worked at the factory. A Mr. D. Shein (I don't remember his first name) was a nice man – he was a spray-painting specialist. Victor Dortheimer was a house painter from Krakow; I had known him before the war. Itzhak Stern, who worked as a bookkeeper, wasn't much of a talker, nor was he a particularly friendly person – he was always busy with his books. Another man I met was Abraham Bankier from Olkusz, Poland. He had been the manager of the Emalia before the war, and Schindler took pity on him and gave him a job. Bankier worked in the Emalia as the chief of the warehouse.

Mr. Wohlfeiler, a sign painter, was a gentle older man. Wohlfeiler's hands were weak, making it difficult for him to paint a straight line with his paintbrush. Schindler knew about Wohlfeiler's problem, so he told me to help him paint his signs and I said that I would do so gladly. Wohlfeiler was a very experienced sign painter and I learned a lot from him. I even learned how to do gold lettering.

The camp at Emalia also had its own Jewish police force, but there weren't many officers on it. The commandant, Zelinger, was a decent man from Olkusz. The Jewish police treated us well because Oskar Schindler had ordered it.

Although life at Schindler's place was a little more humane, as Jews we still weren't free people. We lived with the same rules as in the camp in Płaszów and we were locked up just as we had been there. We didn't have much to wear and what clothing we had was worn and dirty. The small barracks in the camp, located about five minutes' walk behind the factory, were as sparsely furnished as the ones in Płaszów had been. We also lived with terrible nonstop noise, day and night, from large heavy machines in a nearby factory, but after a while I got used to it. We had no choice but to live with it. The truth is that we remained prisoners in a labour camp, but – thanks to Schindler's protection – nobody there was beaten up or killed.

We also worked with Poles in the Emalia factory. Our Polish co-workers were paid employees who could go home to their families and friends at the end of the day – they were free people, free to walk around the streets of Krakow after work. I missed going home to my loving family. The Polish workers were the tradesmen in the Emalia – they had worked there before the war. The Jewish workers were their helpers. The Poles were very helpful to us and gave us news about the war, but they either didn't know about our families or were afraid to tell us the truth. I enjoyed working with the Poles. Through these Polish workers I again started trying to make arrangements to join the Polish partisans.

The enamel factory produced pottery, dinner plates, cups, and pots and pans for the German army and Nazi party members. Schindler sold about 60 per cent of our products on the black market, so he had plenty of money to spend on the Nazi big shots. Schindler bribed Nazi officers and party members with gold, cash, furs and jewellery, and hosted lavish parties with gourmet food, champagne and young, beautiful women. He did all of this to stay in the good graces of the patriotic and fanatical Nazis. Schindler did not have an easy time – he always had to be careful and alert. If he had made any wrong moves with the Nazis, we would all have been dead – including him – but he was much smarter than them.

The Jews at the Emalia were all very lucky that our director was Oskar Schindler. He had charisma and he did a terrific job of watching over us. Determined to keep us away from all danger, he put his own life in danger. In our workplace, we had old people and young people. If they had been in another camp, they would have been killed because, according to the Nazis, they were not productive. But in the Emalia they were protected by Schindler, who made false documents for them. A sixty-eight-year-old man became forty-nine years old. A twelve-year-old boy became fifteen years old. He did the same thing for women and very young girls. There was another man who had only one arm. The Nazis were ready to kill him, but Schindler told them that this man did specialized work on important parts and that he did a delicate job with his fingers. This one-armed man, he told them, was the only man who could do the job. The Jewish man was then safe. Schindler made miracles happen that nobody else could. It is hard to describe how heroic he was. I was so glad that I was transferred to his camp.

At the Emalia, I became Schindler's personal art restorer, retouching all his damaged oil paintings. I loved the artistry of the work and it wasn't a gruelling job. I matched the colours to the old paint to make a damaged oil painting look beautiful again. The task took time, precision, concentration and some knowledge of art painting. I retouched and finished antique furniture as well. My workplace was upstairs next to Itzhak Stern's office. Stern sometimes watched me work and asked, "Are you an artist?" I said, "No, I'm a house painter, but I have some knowledge of art painting." As I've already mentioned, though, Stern didn't talk much. I also did some work for high-ranking Nazis by decorating cups, dinner plates, mugs, and pots and pans with German slogans in gothic letters for birthdays and other important occasions for the Nazis from Berlin.

Schindler was very friendly and always talked to me. He had time for me even though I was a Jew. It was a real pleasure to have a conversation with him. He was a real mensch (a decent and honourable person). He always gave me news about the war, telling me, "Willie, don't worry. The war will be over soon." I knew he wanted to give me hope. I sometimes smoked cigarettes with him – he was a chain smoker – and he always "forgot" to take his cigarettes with him so that I could have them. We sometimes had a small glass of *Schnaps* (fruit liqueur) as well. Oskar Schindler was a wonderful boss. I met his elegant wife, Emilie Schindler, in the Emalia when she came to visit her husband. Schindler introduced us by telling her, "This is Willie, the *Kunstmaler* (art painter)." After being introduced to me as Frau Schindler, she talked to me for a few minutes.

As a member of the Nazi party, Schindler had easy access to high-ranking Nazis, even in Berlin. Amon Göth was still our boss, but Schindler kept Göth away from us. It cost a lot of money, but he did a really good job of it. Schindler was like a father to me and his other Jewish workers. He was always there when trouble came to our people, but I didn't know how long he would be able to protect us from Nazi tyranny and mass murder. He was playing a dangerous game with the Nazis, but I trusted him.

I made some very nice artwork for Schindler. He was pleased, so he came to me with a gift certificate, telling me to take it to the warehouse to pick up my gift. Abraham Bankier, who, as I've said, was in charge of the warehouse, took the paper, looked at it and told me that I didn't need all those things. He gave me a few cigarettes and said, "That's all." So I told him to keep the cigarettes for himself. I told him that I didn't need his charity. I was really angry, so I told him that he was a rotten Jew with no shame and that he was behaving like a small, stupid Nazi. After that, Bankier and I were no longer on friendly terms.

The next morning, I was retouching an oil painting in my workplace when Schindler came in. He was in a cheerful mood and after he said good morning, he asked me how I had liked my gift. I told him that I didn't get it because Bankier had told me that he didn't have those articles in the warehouse. Schindler looked at me with disbelief and disappointment. He told me to come with him to the warehouse. When we got there, Schindler asked Bankier why he hadn't given me my gift and Bankier got red in the face. In front of me, Schindler told Bankier that he hoped this wouldn't happen again. I would get many more gifts, Schindler said, and he was sure Bankier would have enough merchandise in the warehouse to give me them. Then Bankier got all the merchandise that Schindler had ordered for me.

If this incident had happened with another German, Bankier would have received fifty lashes and lost his job or been shot. Bankier was lucky it was Schindler. The bonus I received was very nice – shoes, a shirt, coveralls, cigarettes and soap. I was sure that Bankier hated me now, but I didn't care about him. Although Schindler was a Nazi and Bankier was a Jew, I preferred the Nazi Oskar Schindler.

While I was at the Emalia, Schindler decided to remodel his office, so I did a special job for him. He wanted a natural finish on the wood panelling and didn't want me to use any stain so the wood grain would show through. I'd never done a job like that before, so I had to think about how to do it. I decided to burn the top layer of the wood from the side with a hand torch. The fire caught only the top of the grain, and I was very pleased with the effect. After this part was done, I put three coats of clear varnish on the wood to create a beautiful natural finish. Schindler liked the finish very much, so I got another bonus certificate. I had no more problems with Bankier, but he didn't talk to me – he definitely wasn't gracious when he gave me my bonus.

Another job that I did was to paint a large map of Europe on one of the walls in the big dining room. I had never painted a map of Europe and only had a small printed map to work from, but the job came out professionally and I was happy with my map. Stern even came out of his office to tell me that I had done a nice job and asked me a second time if I was an artist. I told him again that I was a house painter, but that I now considered myself an amateur artist as well.

When I was nearly finished painting the map of Europe, Schindler came straight to me and, pointing to a place on the map with his finger, told me how stupid the Nazis were. They were going the wrong way, he said, and losing ground to the Allied army. He told me that the stupid German army was in disarray and had no chance against the Allies. Schindler was excited and had a smile on his face as he told me this. I didn't know what to say, so I said nothing to be on the safe side.

It was a real pleasure for me to see how happy Schindler was that the Germans were losing on the battle front. He was an inspiration to our people. He gave us hope every day to stay on our feet, to endure our hard lives and hope for a better future. It felt good just being around him.

One day, while I was retouching an oil painting, I overheard a conversation in the office next door. Schindler was saying in a loud voice, "No, I cannot bring your parents from Płaszów – I don't have much power there." A young Jewish woman was in his office, with false non-Jewish identity papers from another country, a free person in Krakow. She was pleading with him and crying, but he said that he couldn't help. The young woman left disappointed, but the next day her parents arrived at the Emalia from Płaszów and their daughter came to visit. What a happy reunion! It was something only Schindler could have done. We were all happy for them.

On another day – I remember that it was a very hot day – I got nervous when I saw an SS unit arrive from Płaszów. They surrounded and entered the Emalia camp to take 10 per cent of our Jewish workers. All the camps affiliated with Płaszów – including ours – had been ordered to send 10 per cent of their Jewish workers to be shot in the main camp. Commandant Amon Göth had given the order and the SS had a free hand to take us because Oskar Schindler was out at the time.

The SS put all the Jewish inmates in a line in front of our barracks and selected who would go to Płaszów. I was one of the "lucky" ones chosen. As the SS army trucks waited to load up the victims, I knew it was the end of me. The rest of the chosen victims and I were all scared and shaken up. We were going to die.

Just then, our luck changed. Schindler's private secretary – the beautiful, good-natured young Polish woman – saw the SS from Płaszów in the camp and called Schindler on the telephone to tell him what was going on. Schindler then called the Emalia guard commandant and gave him the order that no one was to leave the camp until he returned. We really enjoyed seeing the Emalia camp guards watching over the SS so they couldn't take us to Płaszów. But I was so scared. We were all worried about losing our lives.

It wasn't long before Schindler's car sped into the camp like a jet. That was something beautiful to see – Schindler was with us. When he arrived, we felt some hope. But I also knew Commandant Amon Göth only too well. We waited to see whether we would survive or die.

Schindler was both furious and nervous. He took the SS commandant into his car and they drove to Płaszów to speak to Amon Göth. I'm sure that Schindler paid a very high price to get Göth to change his order. Then Schindler and the SS commandant returned to the Emalia and the SS commandant and his men drove back to Płaszów with empty military trucks. We were left behind – alive – in the Emalia camp thanks to our protector Oskar Schindler and his fine Polish secretary. They had saved us from a massacre.

From then on, Göth sent no more such orders to our camp. But other camps affiliated with Płaszów remained in danger because the 10 per cent muster still applied to them. They didn't have angels like Oskar Schindler to protect them.

One morning not long after this terrifying event, Schindler called all the Jewish inmates to a meeting and gave a speech. He told us that he was going to create a strictly Jewish shift of workers at the plant. He wanted to make sure that all the Jewish workers survived and if we were deemed skilled, essential workers we would have more of a chance. As I've explained, up to this point the Jews had worked side by side with the Poles in the plant. The Polish tradesmen worked at the jobs that required experience, while the Jewish workers assisted them. In Schindler's plan, however, a Jewish shift would take over the plant whenever the Nazis came for a big inspection so the Jews would be seen as essential workers. The Polish workers would go home for the day, with pay.

We were very keen to make this clever plan work. We had little experience in making enamel products, but we learned fast from our Polish co-workers. Luckily, we didn't have bad kapos and Nazi sadists to make our lives more difficult. The camp was also only five minutes walking distance from the plant, so we wouldn't have any problem getting there quickly if an inspection occurred with little warning.

We worked conscientiously to produce good work. We didn't want to disappoint our director and protector, Oskar Schindler. We washed all the metals with a strong acid and chemicals and after the washing, put the metal pots, pans, cups and plates into big paint barrels. The paint was heavy and we couldn't use brushes. Instead, using long pliers, we dipped the metal items in and took them out, shook them so that the paint spread evenly, and then took them to the drying area. Using long pliers again, we put the dry pots, pans, plates and cups into a barrel of finishing enamel. When we took them out, we shook the enamel to even it out, took the enamel articles to dry and then baked them in a very hot oven. The people who worked near the oven had to be very strong. The finished products came out beautifully and we felt real satisfaction in the job we had done.

Our people weren't very strong, but they had the will to make this project work. Schindler was proud because the Jewish shift did the best work possible to help him save us. I wanted to show Schindler that we deserved to be saved, that we all appreciated his protection and that we would never let him down, so even in my spare time I volunteered at the plant to help out the Jewish shift.

A large group of Nazis did come from Berlin to inspect the factory. Schindler was smart, as usual. Before the inspection took place, he invited the Nazis to lunch and served them the best champagne and caviar. He gave gifts to the inspectors such as expensive oil paintings, gold, fur coats for their wives and cash. By the end of the lunch, the inspectors were happy and drunk. Schindler knew how to handle the German top brass – the inspection of the factory and camp was a success. Schindler was a genius at saving our lives.

Some time after this, Commandant Amon Göth and his SS man, Green, came from Płaszów to inspect the Emalia camp. Göth and Schindler walked around our camp, with Green following behind. Green wasn't too smart, but he was serious about the inspection and looked for any problem he could find with the Jewish workers. Göth, however, had really come to mooch some cash from Schindler. The inspection was just an excuse.

After snooping around for a while, Green found a Jewish man named Chaskel whom he didn't like. Green told Chaskel to walk in front of him to a large hole in the middle of the camp, then ordered him to drop his pants. Chaskel thought that Green wanted to give him lashes. (Whipping Jews was normal in all other camps but not in the Emalia camp.) While he was waiting for the lashes, Chaskel turned his head and saw Green reaching for his revolver, so he started to run toward Schindler and Göth.

With the revolver in his hand, Green ran after Chaskel, but couldn't shoot because he was afraid that he might accidentally hit Schindler or Göth. When he got closer to Schindler, Chaskel started to cry and said in Yiddish that he was the best worker there and that the SS man wanted to shoot him. Smiling, Göth watched the incident with great enjoyment. Schindler took Green aside and offered him a deal. Schindler told him that he needed Chaskel at work because he was a specialist and offered Green two bottles of *Schnaps* to let Chaskel go free. Green agreed, but said that the Jewish man had to be punished because he had tried to run away from him. Green ordered ten lashes, but Schindler told him that five lashes was enough because Chaskel had to be fit enough to go to work at a hard job. Green agreed to give Chaskel only five lashes. Göth stood nearby watching Green and Schindler negotiate. But Schindler was smart enough to deal directly with Green. If Göth had intervened, the deal would have been very expensive. Schindler was always clever at making deals with the Nazis. Schindler saved Chaskel's life and I was proud of him.

On another occasion, all the Jewish and Polish workers were eating in the factory's dining room. An SS man from Płaszów got very upset at what he saw and started screaming, "Juden raus!" (Jews, get out!) He told the Jewish workers that they had no right to eat with the Poles. It was *Rassenschande*, a racial disgrace. So we had to start eating our lunches outside.

When he found out what the SS man had done to us, Schindler got angry. He gave an order to demolish the dining room, so that all the Polish and Jewish workers had to eat outside. Schindler made sure that, at least in the Emalia, our people weren't humiliated by the Nazis.

One morning, while I was retouching an oil painting, Schindler came into my workplace to lecture me about sabotage. He was very nervous and his face was white. Schindler asked me why I wasn't working and why I wasn't letting others work. I was really surprised to hear him talk to me that way. I knew that he liked me very much. I asked him who had told him such a terrible lie. He said that Victor Dortheimer had reported me to the office. I had known Victor Dortheimer before the war. He had been a house painter like me in Krakow, and he now worked in the Emalia as a house painter. I had done nothing bad to him and was, I thought, on good terms with him, so I had a hard time understanding why he had reported me to the office for sabotage.

Schindler told me that he would normally have to send a report like this to Płaszów and that if Göth received such a report, I would be shot for sabotage. But Schindler was too good and too smart to do this, so he told me to avoid Dortheimer and to not even talk to him. Then Schindler called Dortheimer and told him that he'd better watch his job. He wasn't a foreman or a kapo or my boss. Schindler advised Dortheimer just to get back to work – he didn't want to hear any more complaints from him. Schindler then told me not to talk about this stupid incident anymore, and Schindler's relationship with me returned to what it had been before the "sabotage" incident. I still don't know why Dortheimer did what he did, but I do know that if another German had been in Schindler's place, he wouldn't have questioned me. I would have been guilty as charged and shot for sabotage immediately.

The fact is that Jews did find small ways to sabotage things – often by working as slowly as possible. Schindler knew that we weren't killing ourselves for the Germans. That was okay with him. He understood Jewish feelings toward Nazi brutality. I think that he was even glad, only too happy to keep silent.

There was a small ammunition plant at Schindler's factory. Jewish workers made grenade parts for the German army, but we didn't want to help the Nazi war machine, so as we worked, we did some damage to some of the finished products. We also never produced as much as the plant manager was expecting. He was an evil Nazi – a military type – and our passive resistance made him furious. He prepared a report saying that production was down in the ammunition plant because of Jewish sabotage, and threatened to send the report to Płaszów. That report posed a serious threat to the Jewish workers – we would all be shot – but Schindler got hold of a copy of the report, called the German manager into his office and told him that if he didn't destroy it, Schindler would make sure that he got transferred to the Soviet front. After this incident, the manager actually became friendly to all the Jewish workers. Production – and the same small sabotage – continued as before.

I remember another episode when two house painters were working on the stairwell that went up to Schindler's office. They were lying on the steps because they weren't feeling well, and were talking to me when Schindler came along. He told the two painters that if they didn't feel well, they should come with him and he would give them something to help. I went along, and Schindler gave us all some liquor to drink. It was really good. He told us that we'd be fine now. Any other German who knew that Jews didn't feel well on the job would have shot them.

I was lucky and proud to have known Oskar Schindler and to have worked for him. I will always remember his great help and protection. He will always be my hero and I will always think of him as my best friend. He did much more for us than I could write about. I will never forget him.

KZ Mauthausen-Gusen II

By July 1944, I had been at the Emalia for just over a year when, with the Soviet army advancing toward Poland's borders, Schindler's factory in Krakow had to be closed. The German forces in Poland would now have to deal with the Soviet army, not with unarmed, innocent Jews. I hoped that the Soviet army would avenge us and treat the Nazis the same way that our people had been treated.

As these events were unfolding, Schindler came up with the smart idea of moving the Emalia factory and his Jewish workers from Krakow to his hometown of Brünnlitz in the former Czechoslovakia – this region, known as the Sudetenland, had become part of so-called Greater Germany in 1938.[1] Once Schindler announced this plan, three self-appointed Jewish leaders at the Emalia began deciding who would go to Brünnlitz and who would go back to Płaszów: Bankier, Stern and Marcel Goldberg, whom I called the kapo group or Jewish mafia. I've already mentioned that Bankier was the head of the warehouse and Stern was the bookkeeper; Marcel Goldberg was a Jewish policeman from Płaszów.

Working without Schindler's approval, these three men planned to send about three hundred of Emalia's approximately 1,000 Jews to

---

1 For more on the Sudetenland, see the glossary.

Brünnlitz and the remaining seven hundred or so back to Płaszów. Another seven hundred Jewish prisoners already in Płaszów who could offer them valuables, cash or favours were being chosen to go to Brünnlitz in place of the seven hundred Emalia workers. I wasn't among the people favoured by Bankier and I ended up in the part of the Emalia population that was to be sent to Płaszów – and from there to who knew where.

Schindler didn't know anything about this malicious plan – he didn't actually have anything to do with drawing up the list. He wasn't even in Krakow at the time and he trusted the Jewish trio because he couldn't imagine that they would betray their Jewish co-workers. Schindler – a Nazi – was working hard to save Jews, yet some of our own people were pushing us toward certain death. Bankier, Stern and Goldberg were looking for favours – even favours from young women – or a profit, and they didn't seem to care whether we were murdered. They were behaving like livestock dealers, literally trading us like animals. I was ashamed that Jews could sell us out like merchandise in a market. I tried hard to understand the logic. The Emalia plant and its Jewish workers had to be relocated to Brünnlitz, so I thought that all the Jewish workers at the Emalia in Krakow would go to Brünnlitz with Schindler. We were experienced workers after all.

I knew that Schindler and his Polish secretary liked me and thought that I was an important worker. Whenever they needed help at the plant, I was always there, even to decorate the Emalia products and help the old sign painter Wohlfeiler. I had worked for Schindler as an art restorer and he was pleased with my work. I knew that if they had known what was happening, Schindler and his Polish secretary wouldn't have let me go to Płaszów. But I was so worn down by what was happening that I began to experience that familiar sense of hopelessness – I just didn't care about anything anymore. I was sent to Płaszów with the rest of Bankier, Stern and Goldberg's victims.

It was terribly hot when we arrived in Płaszów near the end of August 1944. The Nazi soldiers screamed at us, pushed us around and beat us. We didn't know whether we were going to stay there or be sent somewhere else. Then I saw a train with cattle cars coming to the place where we were gathered. I had a feeling that the train was coming for us. All the Jews who had come from the Emalia were forced into these cattle cars. It was just like our transport to the Krakow ghetto in the summer of 1942. We were pressed in together so tightly that we couldn't move. We had no bathroom, so we had to urinate where we stood. The smell was terrible. We had no food or water. Just as before, a lot of people in that transport didn't make it – they died in the cattle cars. Because of Bankier, Stern and Goldberg, we headed to our destination: *Konzentrationslager* (KZ) Mauthausen, the huge and notorious camp in Austria.[2]

When we arrived in Mauthausen, we were beaten by the SS guards. As we passed the SS guardhouse at the main entrance, I saw a large and terrible camp with lots of SS men, lots of kapos and lots of barracks. It looked like a city. Then I saw for the first time a big crematorium with smoke coming out of its chimney; it had a terrible smell. The sight of the crematorium operating at full blast left me feeling shaky. I knew that our future was in that chimney and that it was impossible to hide from it. By this point, we all knew what was happening – there was no mistaking that smell.

We were all placed in front of what we knew was a gas chamber and put into columns, long rows four across. Tired, hungry and dirty, we just stood and waited. Then came an order for us to undress completely. Stripped, we stood naked in our columns and waited again. We hoped that we wouldn't be going into the gas chamber or the crematorium, but KZ Mauthausen was a place of mass murder, a place where it was routine to stand stripped before the gas chamber.

---

2 The Mauthausen-Gusen *Konzentrationslager*, or concentration camp, was a large complex made up of about fifty subcamps that operated as both labour and death camps. It was located in Upper Austria, twenty kilometres from the city of Linz.

It looked like we were all ready for our last journey.

We had no choice but to wait for death, anticipating that our miserable lives would end by being pushed into the chamber and gassed. I only hoped it would happen quickly. I didn't want to die then, but we were helpless. Right in front of us, we saw the crematorium; we saw the chimney, and the smoke coming out full blast. It was brutally painful to be so close, to see the smoke rising. Who knew how many victims had died and been burned inside that crematorium?

We then got a new order to each pick up a belt from the place where we had put all our belts. I grabbed one of the belts and put it on my naked body. We all stood like animals in a marketplace waiting to be taken to the slaughterhouse. We had no more strength.

An SS man started to inspect our naked column. I don't know what the inspection was for – I think it was just to humiliate us. When the SS man stopped in front of me, he ordered me to remove my belt. I had to give it to him. I didn't know why he took the belt from me. It was an old belt. He took a small knife from his pocket, cut open the buckle of the belt and found a small gold chain inside the buckle.

With hate in his eyes, the SS man walked around me. I could tell that I had a problem, but what was it? The SS man came closer to me and asked me to hand over the gold watch that should have been attached to the gold chain. Either this SS man was very stupid or he wanted me to suffer more. I was stripped naked and had no place to hide so much as a pin. I tried to explain to the SS man that the belt wasn't mine. I had taken the belt from a pile of hundreds of belts. I had nothing else with me. I think he knew that I didn't have a gold watch.

Then the SS man started getting rough. Screaming "Give me your gold watch," he beat me, kicked me and punched me. I was bleeding all over and in terrible pain. He kicked me in the spine. He started punching my head. Again he screamed, "Give me your gold watch!" He got very mad. He kicked my back again. He kicked me all over my body. I tried to explain, but it was no use.

I was sure that he was going to end my miserable so-called life. He asked me again and again where I had hidden the gold watch. I tried again to explain, but he wasn't in the mood to hear my explanation. He wanted my gold watch – the one that I had never had. That idiot had made up his mind that I had a gold watch. Then he said, "For the last time, give me your gold watch!" With a weak voice, I said one more time, "I don't have it." He could hardly hear what I said.

The SS man took out his revolver, put it to my forehead and said, "For the last time, give me your gold watch or I will shoot you." I knew he was going to kill me, so there was no use talking to him. I was in bad shape – I was half-dead already. After being tortured and beaten and kicked all over my body, I couldn't speak.

An SS-Hauptsturmführer (captain) had been watching the whole show. I'm sure that he enjoyed watching an innocent Jew being kicked around. At this point, he pushed away the SS man, moved close to me and asked the same senseless question: Where had I put my gold watch? I told him that I had never owned a gold watch in my life. If I had had a gold watch, I would have given it to him. I didn't want to lose my life over a gold watch in a place where I had no use for one. The SS officer looked at me from the side and asked me the question one more time. I didn't answer and he pushed me back into the column. I was bleeding badly and in terrible pain. Fortunately, a few of my fellow victims helped me. They told me how the SS officer had pushed the SS man away from me. I had survived another humiliation and somehow avoided death.

Then came the order we'd all been dreading – the order for us to march into the gas chamber. Once inside, we were scared and trembling. We were all pressed together and said our last goodbyes to one another. Then we waited for the gas to come out of the showerheads and looked at the ceiling in anticipation of our deaths. It was torture. A few minutes later, a stream of cold water poured onto our heads. We thought that the gas would come out right after the water, but after about a minute, another order came for us to all get out. The big door opened and, afraid that the Nazis would change their minds, we all started pushing and running toward the open door. It was a panic, but then we were out. We all waited for a new order.

After that horrible incident, we walked in a column to the transit barracks near the crematorium. The smell of burning human flesh and hair was unbearable, and the smell and dirt inside our barracks was foul. Soon it was time for our haircut. The barbers worked at night after a hard day of working outside. They were tired, they weren't professional barbers and they had no professional tools. They were prisoners just as we were. For cutting hair, they got an extra soup. They cut our hair, but in the middle of our heads they shaved a strip an inch wide. We called it the "lice street" – another humiliation.

Then we got our uniforms, grey with blue stripes. We got one jacket and one pair of pants, but no underwear. We also got shoes with wooden soles. We looked like clowns from a cheap circus. Small men received large jackets and big men received small jackets, so we had to exchange the clown jackets among ourselves. It was impossible to get better shoes to move around more easily. We worked and slept in these clothes.

We were taken to a dirty large barracks, where I was surrounded by other miserable inmates who also missed their loved ones. I was still in excruciating pain from the beating I had gotten over the gold watch. Outside our barracks, the crematorium continued in full operation. I saw the smoke come from the chimney and smelled human flesh burning. Who knew who the poor victims were? Some of our relatives or friends? Would we be the next to go up the chimney in smoke?

In the morning, we assembled in front of our barracks for roll call and were counted and checked in case somebody was missing. I soon came to know this routine only too well. After roll call, we were marched to work in a stone quarry in the camp, where we carried granite stones on our backs up very steep steps from the quarry 245 metres below.³ We made about eight or nine trips every day. It was a terribly hard job. We worked seven days a week without food or water. We were tired and miserable and dehumanized. We were covered in lice. To add to our misery, the sun was very strong – it felt too hot to breathe. We didn't know what time it was or what day it was.

We were terrorized. When an SS guard wanted to have fun, he'd kick a victim into the quarry to his death. The victim fell with his stone down 186 steps. I knew one man from Krakow named Ber – a house painter and a friend of my father's – who was kicked down about 160 steps to his death at the bottom of the quarry. Even without being kicked, a lot of people couldn't make it to the top of the steps and fell to their deaths. These steps were covered with human blood – they were known by various names, but we called them "the steps of blood."

There was a cold stream that ran near our quarry, but we were forbidden to go near it. Whoever went near that water was shot. Even knowing that they would be shot, a lot of people ran toward the stream anyway. They couldn't take it anymore, they no longer cared and they were killed.

The SS didn't keep the group that came from Emalia doing construction work long because we were known to be carpenters, painters, stone and brick workers and electricians. One SS man, who was a little friendlier than the others, told me that we were lucky because, being tradesmen, we were needed to work on a big project in Gusen. So, after spending a barbaric three weeks in KZ Mauthausen, I was moved to KZ Gusen II.⁴ The new camp, which was affiliated with KZ

---

3 The Weiner-Graben quarry steps are also known as the "stairs of death." Prisoners at Mauthausen were literally worked to death carrying fifty kilogram stones up the quarry stairs. During the camp's operation, close to 120,000 inmates were killed there.

4 Gusen II, officially called Gusen-Bergkristall-Bau, was established in March 1944, and by September, the camp held close to 20,000 inmates. The lifespan of prisoners

Mauthausen, was another horrible camp. KZ Gusen II looked like a big cemetery. The living and working conditions were similar to those in the previous camp – dirt, brutality, hunger, disease, lice, overwork and the constant threat of mass murder.

When I had arrived at Mauthausen, it was still very hot. Now, the weather changed. After a dirty day of construction work, sometimes in the rain or snow, our prison uniforms got wet and gave off a bad smell. We didn't have any winter clothes. We got very little, awful-tasting food – soup that looked like dirty dishwater and a piece of old bread that was so small it was gone in two bites. The coffee was black, warm water. The food wasn't fit for human consumption and after eating it, we were still hungry.

We didn't have any medicine, doctors or nurses in the camp. If our people fell ill or felt ill, they either died or were shot by the SS. Our end was always close, but as long as we could work for the ruthless Nazis, we could live. We were slaves facing a future of brutal work and beatings. In summer, we worked outside in the heat. In winter, we worked outside in the snow and spent nights in unheated wooden barracks. We sometimes had to stand naked outside our barracks for hours in winter or summer for no reason while the Nazis took pictures of us to show off their heroism to their families and friends at home. I had the feeling that I wasn't a human being any more.

At Gusen II, I was put into Barracks 12 with more than one hundred other Jewish prisoners. The inside of the barracks smelled terrible. There were three tiers of wooden bunk beds with no mattresses or blankets. We slept two or three men to a bunk. Sometimes we slept with people who were already dead.

I was put to work building roads and tunnels in the high hills near the camp for an underground Messerschmitt factory that was manu-

---

at Gusen was generally between four and six months, as they were literally worked to death.

facturing airplanes for the German Luftwaffe (air force).[5] I worked with a power hammer inside the tunnels. After working all day with that big power hammer, I was badly shaken. The work was hard and I had no air to breathe. I also loaded heavy bags of cement.

After I had been in KZ Gusen II for a few days, I met a young Jewish inmate from Hungary. He told me that he had arrived in the camp three months earlier with a transport of five hundred Jews from Hungary – only twenty of them were still alive. The other 480 men had died from torture, murder and typhus. I knew that KZ Gusen II was a horrible camp and I wasn't too surprised to hear what he said, but that was when I realized that there was no chance that I would survive it. I was losing what little strength I had left. I knew that conditions wouldn't get better, and they would likely get much worse in this place of destruction. I didn't know what would happen the next day or next minute. KZ Gusen II was the worst camp that I had ever been in.

One evening, after a long day of working hard on roads in bad weather, I came back to my barracks. Inside, I looked at the ceiling and walls and noticed that they looked very dirty and dark and I started to think about how I could use my trade in order to survive. I decided to talk to our barracks commandant about painting the barracks. His name was Willie, he was a German political prisoner and he was a murderer.[6] Willie had his own room in the back of the

---

5   The inmates at Gusen II were forced to build tunnels to house an underground war-production factory, the Bergkristall, to assemble the Messerschmitt Me262 fighter plane, the most advanced World War II aircraft. For more information, see the glossary.

6   Many Nazi camps had populations that included a variety of non-Jewish prisoners – such as political offenders, communists, homosexuals, or common criminals from Germany and German-occupied Europe. Nazi camp authorities gave certain inmates a higher rank and limited authority to help control the rest of the prisoners. These "privileged" prisoners were called kapos, or barracks commandants. For more information, see "social order within Nazi camps" in the glossary.

barracks. When he was on his way back to his room, I found the chutzpah to stop him and tell him that our barracks was dirty, and that I wanted to paint it to make it look nice and clean. Willie looked surprised that I had had the nerve to tell him that the barracks was dirty, but he must have known that I had told him the truth because he didn't get angry. He asked me if I was a good painter and I answered, "Yes sir." He wrote down my prisoner number and left me standing in the barracks.

Other inmates had been listening to my conversation with Willie. They knew that he killed anybody he didn't like and that he had the power to kill us. A few of them asked me later how I had had the nerve to stop the barracks commandant and talk to him when he was going to his room. They said that I could have been killed and that I had been lucky this time. They told me to be careful with Willie because he was a dangerous animal.

I didn't care. I wasn't sorry that I'd done it. My life was nothing but hard work and suffering. I was humiliated, degraded and beaten by kapos. What did I have to be afraid of? More beatings? I was used to them. I was worse than a slave. Even if Willie had decided to kill me, I was ready. I had nothing to lose. I had already lost all my loved ones.

Early the next morning, we assembled for a dirty cup of coffee – black water, really – and the usual miniature piece of old bread. Then I marched with the others to work in a deep tunnel for the Messerschmitt company. I had initially worked outside on the construction of the roads, buildings and tunnels, and now I was helping to build a warplane in a factory inside the tunnels. It was a terrible job. Because I was a house painter by trade, I had been ordered to spray-paint Messerschmitt's planes in the tunnels. My job was to spray the planes with a cheap, strong-smelling acetone paint. I had a hard time breathing because of the paint fumes from the spray gun and because we had no ventilation in our workplace in the tunnels. The acetone paint was killing me.

I tried to slow down production by blocking the spray guns.

Cleaning a blocked spray gun took some time. I blocked spray guns automatically, without even thinking. When it was possible, other workers slowed down work too. The delays were short and no big deal, but it made us feel a little better about our situation. The other prisoners and I had to be careful not to get caught sabotaging production. We were watched by the SS guards and the kapos. I wished we could really sabotage and destroy the Nazis' war factories.

My boss was a German civilian painter who was about fifty years old. He wasn't so bad for a German. I was lucky – my German boss liked me because I was a painter like him. Sometimes he gave me some bread but only when nobody could see. He was afraid to be seen giving a little food to a Jew. Giving food to a Jew was a crime.

One evening, after a day of hard work in the tunnels in the Messerschmitt factory, I came back to Barracks 12 and was called to our barracks commandant's room. I didn't know why Willie had asked for me – perhaps I was in some trouble. I had forgotten that a few days earlier I had approached him about painting our barracks. I had no choice now but to go to his private room. Inside were three other prisoners, all painting contractors from Krakow I had known before the war. The commandant wanted to question us about our painting knowledge to find out who was the best painter. Why not? For the big price he was paying – an extra portion of watery soup if he was pleased with the work – he could ask for the best workers available. If he wasn't pleased with the work, the pay was murder.

I wasn't prepared for any exams for this kind of work in a concentration camp and I wasn't too comfortable in the presence of the painting contractors from Krakow. But I had no choice. Willie asked me how much chalk calcium we needed to paint our barracks, so I asked permission to check out the place to see how much material we needed. I estimated that we would need three barrels of chalk calcium for spray painting with a machine or two barrels for painting with brushes. The contractors from Krakow disagreed with my estimate. Then Willie asked me how to keep the calcium paint on the wood-panelled walls. (Calcium, like latex, is a water-based paint.) To prevent the chalk paint from getting wiped off the walls, I said that we would need linseed oil or milk, but these were luxury items in a concentration camp. They weren't available. Willie asked for another solution. I said using salt from the camp kitchen would solve our problem.

The painting contractors from Krakow started to laugh and Willie ordered them out. I was glad that I knew about the salt. Painters normally used milk or linseed oil, but I had learned in the technical school in Krakow that we could use salt as a substitute in some situations. So I was the lucky person to get the painting job for our barracks. I only hoped that I would be able to do the job to the commandant's satisfaction.

My estimate was correct, so Willie knew what paint we needed and how much paint we needed. He knew what to use (salt) to prevent the paint on the walls from being wiped off. Then he told me that I would have to do this painting job at night after I came back, tired and hungry, from a hard day of work at the Messerschmitt factory. He promised that I would get extra soup. I was shocked. My whole idea was to work in the camp, not in the factory. I had no choice but to refuse to work at night. To refuse a German order was death, but I didn't even care. If I had started working at night, I would never have finished the job and I would have been killed anyway. So I took a big gamble and said no to a German. I told Willie that I was sorry, but I couldn't paint at night. It was impossible. He didn't say anything to me and left. I was lucky not to be killed.

In the morning, I went back to work at my unpleasant job at the Messerschmitt plant, in that terrible place in the tunnel, where I spray-painted warplanes for the German Luftwaffe. My production was slow. I was lucky that my German boss liked me. He always said, "Du bist ein guter Maler" (You are a good painter), so I didn't have to be so afraid, even though some other Nazis were very bad there. But the strong smell of the cheap paint and the fumes from the spray gun were still unbearable. Sometime later, when I was spray-painting a plane, I fell to the ground unconscious. I didn't know where I was; I was hardly breathing. An SS man saw me lying on the ground, so he took out his revolver to shoot me. That was the Nazi law. If you were unable to do useful work for any reason, you had to die.

My German boss saw that the SS man was ready to shoot me and stopped him. He said that I was his best worker and that he needed me in his workplace. The SS man left, and my boss told some of the other prisoners to take me after work to the *Krankenrevier* (infirmary). I would soon be back at the Messerschmitt plant. When I was taken to the camp infirmary, my co-workers told me the whole story of how my German boss had saved my life. By then I was okay, and I didn't know why I was going to the infirmary, but I was put into the "hospital" in Barracks 13. It was a large barracks and inside, as I've said, there were no doctors, no nurses, no medicines and no beds – just lots of victims lying on the floor. Some were very ill, but some needed only aspirin. I started to feel miserable and panicky in this infirmary where no medical help was available. I could tell that I was in a dangerous place – I felt as if I were surrounded by death. We all seemed to be waiting for a miracle that would never come.

I was very lucky. While I was inside Barracks 13 waiting for medical help, a man I knew came and told me to get out fast because if I stayed I would be murdered with the rest of the poor victims in the barracks. Barracks 13 was about to become a slaughterhouse. He pushed me out through a window. That night, a commando of inmates armed with iron bars and clubs killed between 150 and 200 people in cold blood. The scene inside the infirmary was horrible – blood covered the corpses and flowed out of Barracks 13. The commando committed this brutal massacre in collaboration with the Nazis. They had murdered their fellow inmates to get extra soup. I was lucky – I had been warned and saved by a member of this same commando. I hadn't known this type of situation could exist – I found out the hard way. But the Nazis had many methods to destroy and torture innocent unarmed people. Sometimes they held a victim's head in a pail of water until he died. Living a daily life that was cruel and inhumane, I found myself being grateful to a murderer who saved my life.

After the massacre in Barracks 13, I had no choice but to go back to Barracks 12. I had to take a chance and speak to Willie again. I told him that I was back and that I could paint the barracks. I had the chutzpah to give him my conditions again – I would only work during the daytime. I knew that he was a killer, but I had to take the gamble. Would he kill me? Or would I be lucky to survive for a little while longer? Willie said that I had to go back to work at the Messerschmitt factory. Then I had the nerve to say, "I think that I was almost killed last night in the massacre in the *Krankenrevier* in Barracks 13." Willie looked at me. He smiled a little smile, shook his head and then said okay, I could start painting Barracks 12 in the morning. But when I finished painting, I had to go back to work at the Messerschmitt factory. I agreed. I didn't want to go back, but we lived in this camp on borrowed time, day by day and hour by hour. Being allowed to paint inside the camp during the day was a miracle, and I could only hope that another miracle would come for me later. In the meantime, I knew that Willie wanted the barracks to look its best and that my life depended on this job.

I started to prepare for the painting job, but it wasn't so simple. First, although the day shift went to work in the morning, the night shift came back to sleep during the day. The inmates slept two to a bunk bed at night, but during the time of painting they slept three to a bunk, in one half of the barracks. I had to work out something. Second, I had no tools, no materials and no paint. So I asked Willie to get me a spray-gun machine. (One was available at our neighbouring camp, KZ Gusen I.) I also needed brushes – which were hard to get – and I needed paint. Willie promised a man in our barracks who worked at the Messerschmitt factory extra soup for stealing some paint and a brush. If this worker had been caught stealing paint from the plant, he would have been killed, but his hunger forced him to take the risk and he came in with stolen paint from the factory. We actually managed to get coloured paint! So these problems were solved.

The fact that there were always people sleeping in the barracks made my job much harder. I also had to work without any professional tools. But these were no excuses – the job had to be done. Our camp wasn't a normal place and we weren't normal anymore either, so I couldn't complain.

Willie became a little friendlier to me. He started to like my work and he gave me extra soup, which helped sustain me. Even though the soup tasted like dishwater, I was hungry enough that it tasted all right. When I neared the end of my painting job, Willie asked me if it was possible to make the barracks – especially the kapo room where he was living – more decorative. Was it possible to give some life to it? Once again I had to figure out how to solve the problem of supplies: I had no special tools or different colour paints, but in camp "I don't have it" wasn't an acceptable excuse. You found it, made it or died. The Nazis didn't care what you had to work with. I had to come up with something soon. After all, I was a skilled painter – I had even passed the exam in the camp. So I told Willie that I would try to make something. But what?

I started thinking about what to make in a limited time with limited tools and paint. It was crucial for me to work in the camp and avoid the hard labour, so I had to come up with a solution that would give me the best chance of staying where I was. Working in KZ Gusen II was no picnic (even when I was painting), but it was better than spraying planes with cheap acetone paint. And the reality was that I loved my trade. I had been in the painting trade since childhood. As a youngster, I used to run to my father's jobs after school. I was able to learn about artistic painting and sign painting because my father was good at it. We used to decorate theatres and synagogues. I always took pride in my trade and now it was helping me to survive the Nazi camps.

I came up with an idea to decorate Willie's place. I asked him if he had a penknife and when he said yes I asked him to get me some empty cardboard cartons that the margarine came in from our camp kitchen. He just looked at me, not saying a word. When I had a penknife, the empty cartons and a stone to sharpen the penknife, I had to figure out what décor to make for him and how to make it. I didn't panic.

I started to open and separate the margarine cartons. I cut out about five pieces of the cardboard and created a design, painting the flowers in five colours with leaves in three colours. I used the paint that the other prisoner had managed to steal from the airplane works in exchange for more soup. But my flowers still needed a background. I came up with another idea. I took an old rag dipped in light gold paint, squeezed out the rag and used it to paint the background on the walls. I spread the gold colour on the dado (the bottom of the wall) and the design looked like marble. Then I placed the beautiful carton cut-out flowers with leaves on the walls. Twelve inches separated each flower so the marble background showed nicely. The job looked professional and I liked it very much. Still, even though I had worked hard on that project, there was no guarantee that my crazy boss would be happy with my work when I was finished. I had nothing more to offer. I hoped that Willie would like the job. If he didn't, I would go back to the factory.

Barracks 12 became a model barracks in KZ Gusen II. Willie was so proud that he wanted to show it off and decided to throw a big party for all the barracks commandants in our camp. Even I was proud of my work, and I helped prepare the party. I placed the barracks commandants at their tables and put out the food. They had lots of fine food and alcohol. I don't know how they got it. We could only dream about that kind of food – we hadn't seen it for such a long time. Our barracks commandants didn't eat the same food that we ate. So I was thrilled when Willie told me to go to the table and take some of the delicious food – salami, bread, ham and cake. He said that I would like it and he was right; I liked it very much. I couldn't remember how many years had passed since I had seen such amazing food. It was a very special day for me.

All the barracks commandants were impressed with my painting and told me that I had done a beautiful job. They all wanted me to paint their barracks as well. So I had another chance to stay in the camp instead of returning to the airplane factory. I was pleased with the opportunity and hoped for the best, but I knew that I had to observe the proper protocol, so I said that they should ask for my barracks commandant's permission. They asked and Willie was gratified because they had to ask for his permission to have their barracks painted and because they loved my painting job.

When the commandant from Barracks 10 asked for Willie's permission to have me paint his barracks, Willie gave me the okay, but he also told me not to make any nice designs there. He was proud of his newly painted Barracks 12. He told me again not to make Barracks 10 nicer looking than Barracks 12.

In Barracks 10, I started the work at night because I still had to report for work at the Messerschmitt factory. After a short while, however, my barracks commandant told me not to go to the factory anymore – he told me to stay in camp because I had many more barracks to paint. I was relieved to hear the news. It was an important change for me and I started working days again. When I finished Barracks 10 – a large barracks – the commandant was impressed with my work.

I lined up many more painting jobs. I felt like a proper contractor. During work, the barracks commandant gave me cigarettes and extra food – not much, but it helped. Willie got credit and a lot of gifts such as alcohol, salami and tobacco from the other barracks commandants. Things were a little better and I felt a little better. There were moments when I thought it was only a dream, but it was real. But in KZ Gusen II – as in my former camps – I still had to be alert, lucky and sharp. First, I had to know how to do the various painting jobs they gave me perfectly. The Nazis expected the best. But the most important thing I needed was luck. I was very aware of how lucky I had been to survive until then and I hoped that my luck would continue. If a Jewish prisoner claimed to be a good tradesman – a tailor, painter, carpenter, brick worker and so on – and he wasn't good in his trade, he would be tortured and killed. But even some good tradesmen were killed by inhumane and ruthless Nazis, so nobody was safe there. It didn't matter how good we were or how hard we tried to please the barbaric captors. We had no guarantees that we would survive.

One evening, when the tired, dirty and hungry slaves were coming back from a hard, long day working outside on roads or construction, Willie came into the main barracks and asked for a good carpenter. Some people raised their hands and Willie asked one man who claimed to be a good carpenter if he really was, in fact, a good carpenter. The man answered, "Yes sir." Willie asked the carpenter to make him a nice chair and he said again, "Yes sir."

This poor man promised to make a chair at night after a hard day working outside on the road and was happy at the prospect of getting an extra soup. He had a problem, however, in that he had to make the chair without having any tools or wood. He was in danger. In a few evenings, however, he somehow finished the chair. When Willie looked at the finished chair, he wasn't pleased with the work. He asked the carpenter why the wood didn't have a smooth finish and the carpenter answered that he didn't have any sandpaper. In these camps, however, this was no excuse. Willie said that if the carpenter had used his stupid head, he would have gone outside the barracks, found some broken glass from the windows and used the shards to smooth the rough parts of the chair. Growing angry, Willie said the man wasn't a carpenter. Then Willie picked up the chair and smashed it over the carpenter's head. The blow killed him and the man lay dead in his blood on the floor. He had died for a little extra soup. Willie ordered his body to be taken out of the barracks. The rest of us watched the murder, paralyzed – we couldn't speak. You'd think that we would be used to murder by then. Our people were killed every day in KZ Gusen II.

The Nazis found so many ways to be cruel to Jews. To have fun after a good lunch or dinner, the SS guards came into the camp with leftover food to tease the hungry slaves, throwing bones from meat, rice, potatoes, pieces of cake and cigarettes onto the ground or into the garbage. Starving prisoners fought each other to get the dirty food. The Nazis laughed and took pictures to show to their friends and families in Germany or Austria.

I wouldn't give them the satisfaction. Even though I was really hungry, I wouldn't go near the leftover food. I wouldn't give the Nazis the pleasure of watching me fight my fellow Jews over garbage. It was better to die than to be captured by the Nazis' cameras. I still had a little pride left in me. That was all that I had left and I tried to hold onto it. If I had to die but had managed to keep my pride, then it would be okay.

At the end of March 1945, I had finished all the painting work given to me inside KZ Gusen II and I was given a new job at the infirmary in Barracks 13. A Soviet inmate was performing operations on other sick prisoners in this "hospital." I'm sure that he was a butcher, not a doctor, but in Barracks 13 he acted as a surgeon. He used a large butcher knife on the patients and I now became his assistant surgeon. I knew nothing about medicine. This infirmary was a horrifying place to be. I had the terrible job of assisting in gangrene operations. I stayed near the butcher-surgeon and watched him cut away bad flesh. We had no anesthetic or painkillers – instead, we put a dirty rag in the patient's mouth so that he couldn't scream out loud. The first time that I assisted in one of these operations, I became ill and felt heartbroken. After a few days, however, the job became routine.

Barracks 13 was only open a few evenings a week and only for two hours. After a hard day of work, people who were ill stood outside in a line in the rain or snow or frost and begged to be allowed into the infirmary. They knew if they didn't get better they would eventually be shot. Many of them hoped to be the next one called inside for an operation, but not all of them were lucky enough to get in. Because there were only two hours a night to operate, we couldn't take in all the sick people. Some were disappointed and left with no hope, but we had nothing to offer them anyway.

The situation was tragic. The poor sick prisoners knew that they wouldn't survive without an operation, but I knew that after the operation they wouldn't survive at all because there was no medication and their wounds couldn't be protected or covered. In the morning, after surgery, they would go to work at dusty jobs with open wounds and in terrible pain. They would have to work until they died in their places of work. The operations were a tragic joke on many of the poor inmates, but they always hoped that they would survive. The Poles have a saying that when a person is drowning in deep water, he will grab a sharp razor to try to save himself. The Jewish victims in KZ Gusen II faced a similar choice in the infirmary.

I was also experiencing trouble with my health; I was losing my strength and I felt weak, exhausted and hungry. I was no longer the strong young man that I had once been. I was dirty – I hadn't had a shower with soap in a long time. Every day I witnessed ruthlessness, murder, torture and disease. Every day I saw corpses lying on the ground in dirt. These sights took away a lot of my strength and energy. I missed my loved ones so much that I was in terrible pain. I didn't know if any of them were alive. I hoped that someone – my mother, my sisters, my uncles, aunts, cousins and good friends – had survived.

KZ Gusen II destroyed our people mentally and physically, and the Nazis revelled in their tyranny, barbarism and mass murder. I was sure that this camp would be my last place. I was at the end of my rope. Perhaps I could last a few more weeks, but then it would be all over. There was no chance that I would survive the horror much longer. I needed a miracle to survive.

～

Suddenly, in the middle of April 1945, we were put into long columns four across, surrounded by SS guards and ordered to march the roughly five kilometres from KZ Gusen II to KZ Mauthausen. As we started the hard march, the Nazis screamed at us to go faster. We were all tired, hungry and thirsty. A lot of people died during the march; a lot were shot because they couldn't walk any faster. Then we entered the camp at Mauthausen.

I was afraid that we would have to go to work in the quarry again, carrying the granite stones up the steps. I knew that I wouldn't survive even a few days there. But as it turned out, we were in KZ Mauthausen for only a few hours, and then we were told that we would be going to another camp. We set off on foot again to another camp sixty kilometres away – KZ Gunskirchen.[7]

We didn't know anything about KZ Gunskirchen, but I knew for sure from my previous experiences that we weren't going to a hotel or a picnic. On the way to the camp, we didn't go in columns of four because we could hardly walk. We were lucky that the SS guards got tired too, but we were still beaten up and terrorized and some of us were shot. Marching quickly with the SS guards was a huge struggle. We left many dead people behind on the road.

Somebody on the march pointed his finger to a young girl and told me that she was from Sosnowiec, Poland – he knew that I had family in Sosnowiec. So, as we walked, I moved closer to her for a few minutes and asked if she had met anyone from my family. She said that she was sorry, but she hadn't. Her name was Eva Mrowka

---

7 In April 1945, the Mauthausen camp was overflowing with new inmates who had been evacuated from Auschwitz because of the imminent arrival of Soviet troops there. To alleviate the pressure, prisoners were forced to march to still further camps. The Gunskirchen concentration camp, built in late 1944, was one of the subcamps of the Mauthausen complex. It was intended to operate as a slave labour camp for a few hundred prisoners and was located about seventeen kilometres from the town of Wels, Austria.

and she asked me if I knew anyone from her family, the Traimans, in Wolbrom. I said yes, I knew them well, but I was sorry to have to tell her I hadn't seen them for a long time. Our short talk ended very quickly when an SS man came toward us. We had to separate to avoid getting into serious trouble.

I was really exhausted and hungry. I tried to eat some grass but couldn't stand the taste. I was losing what little strength I had left. My whole body was in pain. With so many of our people dying on the way, I was also losing hope. We were all scared. We didn't know what horror was waiting for us in the new camp. Perhaps the conditions might be a little better there than they were in the other camps – but probably this was just a dream. Yet all we had left were dreams – especially the dream of finding our loved ones alive.

At the end of the exhausting march from KZ Mauthausen to KZ Gunskirchen, half of the people we started with were missing. They weren't with us, so we knew that they were dead. Inside KZ Gunskirchen, we found about 16,000 Jews from Hungary. They had arrived a short time before us – some of them were still with their families and there were even some small children.[8] I was so pleasantly surprised to see Jewish families together, though they were the only Jewish families that I saw together in KZ Gunskirchen. Late in 1944, they had been taken to labour camps, and they were lucky to still be together.

The camp was a horrible place, crazy and filthy.[9] I was in a large barracks with hundreds of tired, hungry slaves and a lot of noise.

---

8   In late 1944 and early 1945, Hungarian Jews from Budapest had been forced to march from Hungary to Austria to be used as slave labour in the Mauthausen complex and Gunskirchen camp.

9   When it was built, the camp was intended to hold hundreds of prisoners, but along with those evacuated from Mauthausen, it actually held thousands when Willie Sterner arrived. Typhoid fever was rampant, and the overcrowded, unsanitary conditions were unbearable.

We saw hardly any food and got no medical help. We had very little water. We didn't have any proper clothing. The lice were terrible. I quickly realized that KZ Gunskirchen was even worse than my previous camps. We had no place to wash and couldn't use the latrines because they were covered in human waste. Nobody was cleaning them. People walked around like zombies and urinated everywhere. The stench was horrible. Our people had lost all sense of pride and dignity; the Nazis had taken it away.

At night, we had to sleep sitting in rows on the dirty mud floor. There was so much overcrowding that we had to spread our legs and each of us sat between another person's legs. All the prisoners had to do the same. In the middle of the night, we sat in this uncomfortable position and pushed and struggled with one another on the muddy floor. It was also impossible to get up, so when we had to urinate, we had no choice but to urinate where we were sitting. Each person urinated on the person in front of him. The picture isn't pleasant, but the Germans had driven us to become animals.

There was another way in which KZ Gunskirchen wasn't like any other camp I had experienced – we didn't have to work. No work in a KZ camp? That was something new. The only work was in the burial commando. One day, I was taken to work with that unit – it was my first burial job there and it was an awful experience. There were a lot of corpses – about two hundred – and we had to throw them by hand into a mass grave. Some of the corpses had some of their flesh cut off; some very hungry and desperate prisoners had resorted to eating flesh from the corpses.

I was in such pain – since my arrival at Gunskirchen I had been repeatedly kicked and pushed and beaten by the SS guards. I had been punched in the face many times. I was depressed. I didn't know what was going on with me. I was still a young man, but I was now broken morally and physically.

The whole camp was in disarray. We received no orders of the day but still a sense of powerlessness was everywhere. The hunger, torture, beatings and sadism continued. We weren't alive – we merely existed. Our people were dying so fast that the burial commando couldn't keep up. The camp population fell by more than half. A lot of corpses lay on the ground amidst urine and human waste.

And then – one day – the Nazis started to disappear. Why?

Liberation

May 4, 1945 – a day of joy and hope. I saw the SS commandant in KZ Gunskirchen put a white flag on his car, but I didn't know why. I heard cannon shots and artillery fire, but I thought that the Nazis were having military training. I didn't think that help was coming our way and I still didn't know that the US army was very close to the camp.

Our commandant drove his car with the white flag in the direction of the cannon shots. I thought that he was going to his headquarters. One of the SS guards told me that the commandant had received an order to blow up the camp, but at the last minute he had decided not to follow it. All the commandant would have had to do was give a command for the explosives to be set off and the lives of thousands of innocent Jews would have ended. Instead, he drove his car with the white flag toward the approaching US army and gave himself up. He hoped to receive a lesser charge for the crimes he had committed against our people in that horrific camp.

In the late afternoon, I saw a number of US military trucks passing the camp. Inside the camp, we all became very emotional. Wild with happiness, our people began crying, dancing and screaming. We screamed that the ugly war was over and that we were a free people. We were free of our pain and of the Nazi murderers. Some of our people who still had the strength started to dance outside the barracks. The emotion of that day is difficult to describe. We hoped that it all wasn't just a beautiful dream.

We stood inside the camp near the barbed-wire fence and, looking through the wires, we watched the US army pass about ten metres away from us. But some of the German SS guards were still at their posts, so we became a little confused. We were no longer sure what was happening. Maybe the war was over and maybe it wasn't. Everyone – the Jewish prisoners, that is – was very happy and scared at the same time. Maybe the Nazis would come back. (God forbid!) We looked for somebody from outside the camp to give us some assurance that the war was indeed over. But nobody came.

It felt as if everyone in the camp had become part of a close-knit Jewish family, born at the same time. We all thought about the same thing: our loved ones. Would we see them again? Would we be happy again? What kind of future would we have? But we also saw how a lot of our people were dying, even now. Unlike us, they never got the chance to be free. It was painful and tragic to be surrounded by so many corpses.

The German guards became less and less visible. We still weren't sure that the war was over. We were still waiting for someone from the real world to tell us the good news, to tell us that the war was over, to tell us, finally, that we were free. But still nobody came. We were all so mixed up. We weren't sure of anything. We were so exhausted and so hungry. While the others watched the US army trucks pass by the camp, I found myself a free corner in the barracks so I could get a little sleep. I thought that if the US army was here to stay, I would see them in the morning. I wasn't as happy as some other prisoners were; I wasn't as excited as others to celebrate my freedom. I was in a kind of dreamy melancholy.

Above all, I wanted to learn news about what had happened to my loved ones. I hoped that there would be good news, but I was afraid of what I would find out. I didn't know if I would see my family again. Was there anyone of my dear family left to be liberated too?

The next morning, on May 5, we continued to watch columns of US army trucks pass by the camp. We still stood behind the barbed-wire fence. We were still watched by a few German guards. The US soldiers and other free people still hadn't come into the camps, and we still hadn't received any official word about the war, so I remained unsure about our freedom. People were dying in camp because they weren't getting any medical help. We had no help at all. We had to decide ourselves whether to stay in the camp or try to leave.

I wanted to taste the freedom that we were dreaming about. Some of us decided to take a chance and went to the main gate. An old German soldier was on guard there, but he didn't try to stop us. Confused, some of us went outside the camp. We didn't know what to expect or where to go. Many other people didn't leave the camp because they were afraid that the Nazis would come back. Most of our people were too ill to leave. People were depressed and indifferent. Most of us no longer even had the capacity to grasp the meaning of freedom.

That day, though, on May 5, 1945, I finally realized that we had indeed been liberated from KZ Gunskirchen by the 71st Division of the US army under the command of Major General Willard G. Wyman. I was a free young man, but – like most of our people in the camp – I wasn't normal. My mind was foggy. Nothing was clear to me. Who was I now? And what was I? A forgotten Jew from a terrible concentration camp. I had nobody. I was all alone.

I couldn't figure out how I had survived so many concentration camps. I had entered my first labour camp in Pustków-Dębica in December 1940, and I had worked as a slave labourer under the Nazis until May 1945. I had experienced hunger, thirst, beatings, terror, oppression, humiliation and barbarism. I had seen mass murder and ruthlessness. I had worked long, hard hours in all kinds of weather. How had I survived that horrible ordeal? I wasn't the strongest man or the smartest man among the survivors. I was lucky that I was liberated on May 5, 1945. If liberation had come even one week later, I would probably have been dead. I survived that terrible hell because I was lucky.

All the liberated prisoners were hungry, dirty and full of lice. We were homeless and we didn't know where to go. We were also very lonely – we didn't know what had become of our families. Along with our freedom came sorrow and pain that would be with us forever. Conditions, however, got much better for us over time. The US army and some US civilian organizations started working very hard to help us. I was grateful for their help and began to see a glimmer of hope.

Many thousands of our people, however, never got the chance to experience freedom. After suffering so many bitter years of Nazi terror and so much pain, after suffering overwork, beatings, starvation, illness and Nazi tyranny, they died of illness, suicide and malnutrition in the days of liberation. They were simply too weak to stand on their feet.

On the afternoon of May 5, I left Gunskirchen and started to walk – if I could call it walking – to the nearby city of Wels. Other survivors who had the same will to taste freedom came with me. We started to walk slowly. On the way to Wels, US soldiers in columns of army trucks threw cans of cold meat, cigarettes and chocolates to us. We looked like beggars and we were very hungry; they were trying to help us. We hadn't eaten any food for a few days, so on the way to Wels people started eating the canned meat. They ate too much meat too quickly – their weakened digestive systems couldn't handle such rich food after years of starvation – and many people died from it. The US soldiers didn't understand the condition the survivors were in, but I was nonetheless grateful to them for their goodwill and generosity.

Later that night, while I was walking through the dark streets of Wels, a city I didn't know at all, two US soldiers came out of nowhere. One of them asked me if I was from Poland, and when I said yes in Polish, he started to ask me questions. Why was I on the street so late at night? I told him that I had no place to go, so the soldier who had spoken to me in Polish said that they – the Americans – hadn't fought the Nazis so that I, after all that I had suffered from the Nazis, should walk in the dark streets. The other soldier watched but didn't understand what we were saying. Then the two soldiers told me to follow them. They took me to a very nice Austrian home and, in broken German, told the Austrian woman who lived there to give me some good food and a warm bed to sleep in. She was afraid of the US soldiers and immediately answered, "Yes, sir." The soldiers told her that if she didn't feed me well and allow me to get a good night's sleep, she would be shot. I went into her very clean home – I hadn't seen one for a long time – took a long hot shower and ate a good meal. I stayed with the Austrian woman for two days and she was very pleasant to me. I started to feel a little better.

While I was in the Austrian woman's home, I heard that a Displaced Persons (DP) camp would be opening soon in Wels. Survivors would be able to stay there and the United Nations Relief and Rehabilitation Administration (UNRRA) would take care of us.[1] When I left the woman's home, I thanked her and, smiling, the woman wished me good luck. I then made my way to the Lichteneck DP camp in Wels.

A few days after I got to Wels, I came down with typhoid fever. I was very weak and couldn't stand up. I felt as though my whole body was on fire, and I was sure that I wouldn't survive much longer. Some people (I don't know who they were) moved me into a temporary hospital in a large barracks with other ill survivors. I was placed on a cement floor covered with a little straw. There wasn't much air to breathe and no water to drink. The smell of urine was strong. It was a terrible place.

An Austrian doctor was in charge of the hospital and he came to examine me – probably to see if I was alive. I was hot and thirsty, and

---

1 The UNRRA assumed responsibility for the administration of the DP camps and helping refugees after the war. For more information on DPs, DP camps and the UNRRA, see the glossary.

in a very weak voice I asked the doctor for a little water. The doctor looked at me as if I were crazy and said in a loud voice, "No water for you." I thought that he must be a Nazi. I tried asking for water again, but my voice was too weak. I couldn't move and my fever was so high I was sure I was dying. I was sure this was the end of me. Nobody cared. Nobody offered me any help. While I lay on that cement floor like a future corpse, I began to believe that my freedom would be short-lived.

A few hours later, a US army officer came in. Luckily for me, he was also a doctor. He looked over all the patients and, when he got close to me, saw the condition that I was in. Because I didn't speak any English, I asked him in German to please give me some water. It turned out that he spoke some Yiddish – he was Jewish! He turned to the Austrian doctor and ordered him to give me as much water as I was able to drink. The Austrian doctor looked surprised but very soon I got the most important gift of water. This little water was a lifesaver – it tasted like the best champagne. It gave me a little hope and I felt better. I began to think that I might survive because of the Jewish American doctor's help. He gave me hope too.

Unfortunately, despite getting some water, the high fever loved me too much and stayed with me much too long. I didn't have much life left in me. A lot of people like me died in that barracks hospital after the war. Liberation came too late for them.

After suffering from typhoid for many weeks, however, I started to get a little better and a little stronger. I could stand up by myself. But I still had one major problem – I couldn't eat. I wasn't hungry at all. In broken Yiddish, the Jewish American doctor told me that he had no medicine for me – I would just have to force myself to eat. If I didn't eat, I had no chance of surviving. He told me to fight to get my strength and health back. It would be such a tragedy, he said, if I gave up after suffering so much.

I knew that my doctor was right, so I promised him and myself that I would try to eat. I would eat even if I didn't like the food. So I started to force myself to eat small meals. I tried very hard and didn't give up. I slowly got stronger. I was lucky that I got such good care from a Jewish doctor. We understood each other well. Even though he didn't have much in the way of medication, he did the best under the circumstances and helped me and the other ill survivors. Thanks to my doctor, I got well again. But once I recovered, the fact that I was alone in the world with no future started to weigh on me again.

Chief of the Jewish Police

Soon after my recovery, I moved back into the DP quarters in Lichteneck in Wels. The camp had large barracks made of wood. The camp survivors were still dirty and full of lice – even though I washed myself a few times every day and changed clothing often, I couldn't seem to get rid of the lice. We may have been free of the Nazis, but we weren't free of the lice – they remained to torture us. I found a German army building outside the DP camp that had a store of all-new German army uniforms and underwear. I threw out my old lice-ridden clothes, washed myself many times and changed my new German uniforms and underwear daily. It didn't help. I couldn't get rid of these Nazi parasites and I didn't know how else to fight them. They were eating me alive. It made me feel dejected and ashamed.

Some days later, US soldiers came to the Wels DP camp and told us to line up outside our barracks, that they would help us get rid of the lice. I wasn't so sure that anybody could help, but the soldiers, who were armed with spray guns, sprayed DDT powder all over us.[1] I didn't know what DDT was – all I knew was that the Americans said

---

1 DDT, short for dichlorodiphenyltrichloroethane, is a strong chemical that was widely used as a pesticide and to control the spread of disease after 1939. It is now banned in many countries.

that DDT would rid us of the plague and they were right. It worked like magic. No more lice! I felt more human and freer to meet regular people. I was grateful to the US army for saving everyone in the DP camp from such torture.

The DP camp in Wels, like many others, was under the management of the UNRRA, and the DPs and survivors also received help from the American Jewish Joint Distribution Committee (JDC) and other Jewish organizations in Canada.[2] They worked hard to normalize our lives, to get us back on our feet and build a future. I appreciated – and still appreciate – the efforts of those good, dedicated people and the enormous help that we got from them. There was also a small Jewish committee in Wels that administered our camp.

The people in our camp were from many different countries. We were living in DP conditions, so life wasn't exactly normal, but at least we weren't in a Nazi concentration camp. We were free people, we had enough food to eat, we weren't being deliberately humiliated on a regular basis and – finally – we had no more "Nazi" lice. Compared with the terrible places we had come from, this camp was heaven. I lived in a large room that I shared with other Holocaust survivors. We hung blankets from the ceiling to divide the room and give each other some privacy. There were ten survivors – some married and some single – in this room, so we had to do our best to make the living conditions as pleasant as possible for everyone. We kept the place clean and managed very well.

We came to be like a family. We needed each other – we were all very lonely and hungry for friendship – so we all did our best to get close to one another. We shared our pain about the terrible past and our uncertainty about our loved ones. I tried to be cheerful and hoped that we would have a better future with our families and

---

2   The American Jewish Joint Distribution Committee (JDC), is a US aid organization that was also known colloquially as the "Joint." For more information, see the glossary.

friends. I also met a lot of US soldiers who spoke Polish – I was very glad about that because I didn't speak any English – and some of us became good friends.

About a month after I arrived in the DP camp in Wels, in early June 1945, the UNRRA director asked me to organize a Jewish police department and I soon became the chief of fourteen volunteer police officers. The work was good for me – I was busy with my new job and had less time for sorrow. My police department was made up of Jewish DPs and our job was to help our people with their daily problems and keep law and order among our people. We also watched for strangers who came into the camp. We did our police work with ability and goodwill, and things ran very smoothly.

I began looking for news about my family through the Red Cross.[3] I knew the search wouldn't be easy, but I hoped that I would be lucky enough to find them. It was so difficult for me to be without my loved ones. A lot of the time, I was moody and lonely. I was filled with pain and sorrow. Bad memories haunted me and I had a hard time sleeping at night. I dreamed terrible dreams about the Nazis, and when I awoke I was soaked with sweat. I tried to push away the Nazi horror. I wanted a normal life, but it wasn't so easy. I was having a hard time adjusting to freedom. I hoped to get out of Austria quickly but I wasn't sure where to go.

Meanwhile, the best way for many of the men in the DP camp to deal with their loneliness seemed to be for them to seek out the companionship of young, friendly, good-looking Austrian women. Many of the younger men started to look for social events where they could meet young women, and the young Austrian women seemed to like the young Jewish men. Even the older Jewish men ran after

---

3 The International Committee of the Red Cross, based in Geneva, acted as one of the main agencies in Europe during and after the war for locating and getting information about missing people, and in particular about Jews and concentration camp inmates.

young Austrian women. In fact, the situation soon got to be out of control. To me, the DPs looked like wild people who had found freedom but didn't even know how to behave. I understood why the men needed friendship, especially the companionship of young women, but I didn't understand why such beautiful Austrian girls liked our men so much. They knew that Jewish male survivors didn't have any money or valuables – they didn't even have nice clothes to wear. We were all living in a DP camp and except for food and used clothing, we had nothing. We couldn't invite Austrian girls to where we were living or even offer them coffee. But the Austrian girls didn't demand anything from our men except companionship. They were happy to be with our men, and our men were happy to be with them. Some of them later got married and some of the young Austrian women converted to the Jewish religion and brought up their children in the Jewish faith.

Some of the young Jewish women who had survived the horrors of the camps, on the other hand, were more demanding of our men even though the men didn't have much to offer. In all the DP camps, a rumour went around that the young Jewish women were asking the Jewish men if they had stopwatches, officer boots and diamonds. I don't know how true the rumour was – maybe it was true – but a lot of our men married Austrian women because of the rumour. Maybe the rumour was just a good excuse!

As they arrived, the refugees in Wels were moved into a DP facility that was housed in a large building in Wels called Herminen Hof (Hermine's Court). A few months after I got there, a young woman came to the camp to visit some of her friends and as soon as they saw her come into the room, they all started screaming and crying and kissing one another. I didn't know what was going on at first, and then I realized that what I was seeing was a joyous reunion. I was happy for them. After they all sat down, excited and tired, the young woman turned to me with a nice smile and said, "Hi, Willie!" I was really surprised. I had never seen her before. Where did she know me from and how did she know my name? She saw that I was puzzled, so she came closer and reminded me that we had met on the terrible march from KZ Mauthausen to KZ Gunskirchen.

She was beautiful. She had blond hair, wore a white dress and had a friendly smile. Her name was Eva Mrowka and she was from Sosnowiec, Poland. On that march, however, she hadn't looked as beautiful as she did now. She had looked like a beggar – dirty, tired and hungry (and I had looked the same). I had hardly noticed her beautiful face. I was glad to see her as a free young woman in a better place than Gunskirchen, to meet her again in the DP camp. But I would never have recognized her. On the march from Mauthausen to Gunskirchen, I had been miserable and hadn't paid any attention to women, but in the DP camp I certainly did pay attention to Eva Mrowka. She had just come out of hospital where she had been recovering from lengthy illnesses, including typhoid. She was planning to stay in the DP camp in Wels with her friends.

Eva and I became very close. We were both alone – neither of us had any family there – and I saw her often. A year after the end of the war, in June 1946, we made plans to marry. Together we prayed to God to give us back our loved ones. I hoped that we would find them soon so we could be truly happy again.

Some months after Eva arrived in Wels, I received a visit from a very distinguished old friend from the Krakow Emalia – Oskar Schindler. I was delighted to see such a good friend – my angel – and introduce him to Eva. I was sorry that I couldn't even offer him a coffee – I didn't have anything to offer him. But I was glad to talk to him about the times in the Emalia, our work and especially my work for him.

Schindler wasn't the same man that I had known in the Emalia. He never smiled. His spirits were down. He had lost his charisma. He no longer had any special work, such as preventing as many Jews as possible from being harassed or beaten up by kapos or the SS. He no longer had to stop sadists such as Płaszów's Commandant Amon Göth from humiliating and killing innocent unarmed Jews. Schindler looked like any other DP. He was no better off than I was. He was no longer the optimistic man I had known. What a terrible change for such a fine person! I felt very sorry for him.

Schindler asked me if I had found any of my family or former workers from the Krakow Emalia. I told him that I had found no one until now, but still hoped to find my family. I saw sorrow on his face. He told me that he was glad that I wasn't alone in the camp and that I had found a fine and lovely young lady. He hoped that Eva and I would be happy together.

I asked Schindler about the transfer of Jews from the Emalia in Krakow to Brünnlitz, and about the inhuman exchange of Jews between the Emalia and the camp at Płaszów. Schindler told me that he hadn't been involved in the exchange – he had been too busy with the new place in Brünnlitz. It had all been organized by Bankier, Stern and Goldberg. Schindler told me that he was sorry about everything that had happened. I knew that he hadn't made the list – he didn't need a list. We were all registered at the Krakow Emalia and if he had made a list, he would have chosen me to be first on it.

Schindler didn't know what his future would hold and he didn't have any place to go. He told me not to worry; he would find something somewhere. The time of our get-together ended. We hoped for a better future and to see each other again, then we said our goodbyes and he left. I tried to find him years later, but it was impossible for me. I would have needed money to travel, which I never had, and I didn't even know what country he was living in.

Oskar Schindler was our saviour. Thanks to his hard work and determination, he saved about 1,200 Jewish lives from torture and starvation and death. Risking his freedom, he did the impossible to save our people. He will always be my hero and I will never forget him. If we had had more Oskar Schindlers, many more of our people would have been saved. He deserved a much better life. I hoped that our Jewish institutions would take special care of him. In my opinion, he should have been treated like a king for what he did for us. I hoped that we – the Jewish people – would show our gratitude and thanks for how hard he worked to save us. He was one of a kind; he deserved the best of the best.[4]

In the spring of 1946, we moved from the DP camp in Wels to a new DP community in Linz-Bindermichl, Austria. About 2,500 people lived there – among them survivors from the concentration camps, as well as people who had survived in the Soviet Union, partisans and freedom fighters. I didn't see members of my family but still hoped to find them one day.

The new camp in Linz-Bindermichl had large modern buildings, and each apartment had a modern kitchen, a bedroom, a bathroom and a hall. We had hot running water and could take showers. It was a nice place for DPs. We kept our place as clean as possible and felt more human there. We had a Jewish amateur theatre, Zionist organizations, a Jewish sport club, a mikvah (ritual bath), an Organization for Rehabilitation through Training (ORT) trade school, a drivers' school and a Jewish committee. Compared to the hell I had come from, this place was luxury.

The Jewish committee took care of the DP community in Linz-Bindermichl. The president was a gentleman named Mr. Spokojny, the secretary was Mr. Shuss and the police commissioner was Dr. Knoll, a lawyer. The commandant of the police department, Jozef Sterngast, was a man I had known in Krakow before the war, a good leader and a fine man. All these men worked hard at their jobs.

I joined the Jewish police in Bindermichl to keep law and order

---

4 After the war, Oskar and Emilie Schindler lived in Germany until 1949, at which time, under constant threat from former Nazis, they fled to Argentina. Schindler returned alone to Germany in 1957 and divided his remaining years between Germany and Israel. He was honoured and supported by Jewish survivors whom he had saved, and by organizations in both Argentina and Israel. He died in Germany in 1974 and in 1993 Yad Vashem posthumously awarded Oskar Schindler the title "Righteous Among the Nations" for his courageous efforts to save Jews.

and to keep our people safe and out of trouble. Although I had never graduated from a police academy, I had been interested in police work in Poland before the war. I read a lot of books about criminals and police, so I had a little knowledge, and experience came to me on the job. I soon was nominated chief of the seventy-five Jewish volunteer policemen and five staff officers. As police chief, I had important duties and quite a lot of responsibility. I got some great help and support from the US military police (MPs), the US Criminal Investigation Division (CID, now known as the US Army Criminal Investigation Command) and from the Austrian police. I learned a lot from them and managed my Jewish police department well. I even carried a revolver; I got my permit from the US Counter Intelligence Corps (CIC).

My officers were disciplined, dedicated and honest. They didn't carry weapons. Each police officer wore a blue-grey uniform with the Star of David on his hat and, on the left arm of the uniform, a blue insignia on a white background with a small gold Star of David. In Bindermichl the Star of David wasn't the Nazi star of humiliation – it was a symbol of our pride and dignity.

It wasn't easy teaching the men how to behave on duty as proud police officers. I had to train them to come to work clean-shaven, to wear clean uniforms and clean shoes, and to be polite but firm with people. At first, I had a problem with the fact that the force included men from several different countries who spoke different languages. But even this problem was resolved through good will and effort by everyone.

There were many depressed survivors in Linz-Bindermichl, people who had lost their loved ones and all hope of finding them alive. The police officers didn't have an easy job dealing with them – emotions often ran high in the camp. We had to be friendly and helpful but firm. It helped a great deal that people trusted and respected us. I was very proud of my Jewish police officers.

In my role as chief of police I worked closely with the Bindermichl

Jewish committee and with the US and Austrian authorities. I had no problem communicating with the Austrians because I spoke some German, but I had a difficult time working with the US MPs and the US intelligence officers of the Office of Strategic Services (OSS), as well as with the UNRRA authorities, because I didn't speak any English. I was able to manage better once they found me an interpreter. I had no problem communicating with the CID because one of their officers – Ted Ciekanski from Chicago – spoke Polish very well. He helped me both with police work and by serving as a liaison between our police department and some of the American police departments. We became good friends and saw each other socially. I also had close contact with a Jewish MP from Brooklyn. We spoke Yiddish, so I didn't need an interpreter.

As was true throughout much of Europe in the immediate postwar period, Bindermichl had a large organized black market, or underground economy. It was illegal, but I didn't bother the black marketeers. What I wasn't looking for, I didn't know about. As far as I was concerned, the black market didn't exist in Bindermichl.

We also had Zionist organizations, some of which were considered illegal by the Allied occupation authorities, such as the Bricha and Irgun. The Bricha worked to transport Jews to pre-state Israel. In our community, the Bricha leader was a man named Abraham, who was a very hard-working man. The Irgun – which was part of the Jabotinsky movement – fought to establish a Jewish homeland in what was then British Mandate Palestine.[5] The US and British

---

5   Bricha was the name given to the clandestine migration of Jews from Eastern Europe and DP camps to pre-state Israel following World War II. The Irgun, a militant Zionist organization that existed between 1937 and 1948, was founded and commanded by Ze'ev Jabotinsky and was guided by the ideology of Revisionist Zionism and, in particular, of the right to bear arms to defend Jews and establish a Jewish state in Palestine by any means necessary. For more information on Bricha, the Irgun, and Jabotinsky and Revisionist Zionism, see the glossary.

governments called the Irgun a terrorist organization, but to me its members were heroes.

When I was in the concentration camps, my dream – if I survived – was to see Germans standing at attention before me as I had had to stand, humiliated, before them. I wanted to recover my self-esteem and my dignity. I was therefore very proud on the day that some of my Jewish police officers and I went to a memorial service in Salzburg, Austria and marched through the streets in our Jewish police uniforms, flying the blue-and-white flag with a Jewish star that would soon become the flag of the State of Israel. Many of Salzburg's police officers stood at attention and saluted us and our flag as we passed. That gave me tremendous pleasure – that day, I felt that we regained our pride and dignity as Jews.

To the same end, I ordered half our Jewish police force to march in the city of Linz in their blue-grey uniforms every day, displaying the beautiful Star of David on their caps and on their left arms. One of my officers proudly carried our blue-and-white flag. My Jewish police officers marched in many Austrian cities including Wels, Bad Ischl and Bad Gastein. In Linz, the high-ranking Austrian police officers saluted me and addressed me with full respect. When they came to my office for police business, they stood at attention until I told them to relax. I had become the chief of a well-respected Jewish police department.

One day, I was invited to meet the Austrian director of the Linz police department. When I went into his office in my Jewish police uniform, all the high-ranking staff officers stood at attention. The director came to me, instead of waiting for me to come to him, we shook hands and then we got down to our police work. All these gestures helped me regain my sense of dignity after all I'd been through.

The Linz police director was a pleasant man about fifty years old and a smart police officer. He was in charge of a large police department that was well-equipped and well-organized. He gave me some important tips about police work and helped me a great deal. One day, I got a telephone call from him asking for my help in solving a sensitive issue that had become a problem in Linz. Both Austrians and survivors waited in line for the buses at a bus stop near Linz-Bindermichl. Austrians paid for their tickets, but the survivors didn't have to pay and didn't want to stand in line – they were pushing past the paying passengers to get on the buses. This had developed into an unpleasant, strained situation. Unfortunately, the survivors' horrific experiences in the concentration camps had made them forget how to behave in the civilized world.

The Linz police director asked me to do him an important favour. Although the bus stop wasn't in my territory, he asked me if I would agree to post Jewish police officers there for a short time. The director said that he could put Austrian police officers there, but that might cause even more trouble because the Jewish survivors would not take orders from the Austrian police and he didn't want to have to use any force against them. He thought that the survivors would have more respect for Jewish police than for Austrian police.

I understood the problem right away. Our people were extremely sensitive to being ordered around by any German or Austrian police. We had suffered so much pain from our treatment before and during the war, we still suffered so much from that pain, and we would continue to suffer from it for the rest of our lives. I had no choice but to help him out in order to protect our people. I didn't want them to be harmed or subject to force by the Austrian police. So I ordered some of my Jewish police officers to stand at the bus stop.

When they saw the Jewish police the survivors were pleasantly surprised because they had expected Austrian police to keep order at the bus stop. The Jewish police officers instructed all the passengers at the bus stop how to behave in a public place in a large city and to be respectful of others – in short, to be human again. The Jewish police officers performed well at this difficult job and finished their work at the bus stop in only four weeks.

After the situation was well under control, I received a telephone

call from the Linz police director expressing his thanks and appreciation for a job well done. The Austrian passengers were also grateful to
the Jewish police for their good work at the bus stop. My dream had
come true – the Austrian passengers had gladly followed the orders
of the Jewish police officers. I was extremely proud of my Jewish police department – they had performed well and gained the respect of
both the Austrian community and the survivors.

There were still some Nazi fanatics in Linz, so I couldn't take any
chances with the safety of our people. In addition to that, we had
the usual problems with thievery. Our community in Bindermichl
was an open place with open entrances and each building had three
floors. I put my police officers on twenty-four-hour patrol duty to
protect the survivors from any harm. I ordered signs for all the outside entrances saying that overnight visitors had to register at the
Bindermichl police station. The order was signed by Willie Sterner,
chief of the Jewish police department. Registration was free of charge
– all the visitor had to do was see the police officer on duty and give a
name and an address. The visitor's ID card would remain at the police
station until the next morning, at which time the visitor would come
with someone who could serve as a guarantor by signing a document
saying that all the information was correct. Then the visitor was free
to go. The Jewish police had to know who was coming into the community from the outside.

I had received a few reports from my staff officers of thefts of
goods such as gold watches, money and cigarettes. While I was reading the reports, I started to get suspicious because all the reports had
come from single men. I was sure that the thefts had been committed
by female visitors who were staying overnight and taking goods in
exchange for "services rendered." When I called a meeting with my
staff, I heard that these thefts had been going on for a long time and
we made a decision to take stronger measures to enforce the registry
of overnight visitors at the police station.

I ordered my staff police officers to start visiting the suspected single men's apartments at night. After a raid, we arrested fifteen or twenty unregistered young women from Linz. The police officers took them into custody and kept them at the police station overnight. One of the staff officers called the MPs or the Austrian police, who took the women away to be examined for venereal disease by an Austrian doctor. Our raid on their apartments forced the young men in our community to learn to respect our laws the hard way.

As I've said, the DPs in Linz-Bindermichl were from many different countries in Europe and spoke different languages. Most had come from concentration camps, but some of them had come from the Soviet Union, some were partisans, and some had been saved by heroic Polish people. They were all survivors. Many of them had a hard time adjusting to normal life and some didn't even understand why we had a Jewish police force, but they quickly learned. We explained that the Jewish police were there to protect all Jewish survivors from harm. We watched for outsiders who came into our community and we kept law and order. We resolved problems between neighbours who played loud music after eleven o'clock at night and people who wanted to sleep. If anyone in our community was arrested by the Linz police, I would intervene so that our people were protected by our Jewish police department. The Jewish police also prepared our people to live in a normal, free society.

There was a large partisan organization in the Linz-Bindermichl community. Its leaders, Mr. Lewin and Mr. Zlocowski, were decent people, but some of their members behaved as if they were still partisans and had their own laws. A few bad apples got out of control and started to behave like a mafia. They held up people at night, broke into private homes, beat up people and took away their cigarettes, chocolates and other items. They terrorized our people.

I organized a staff meeting and we investigated the incidents. We found out that two male suspects were members of the partisan group, but we didn't know their names. I called Lewin and Zlocowksi into my office and said that if they couldn't control their members, I would be forced to shut down their organization and activities. The two leaders asked me to come to a partisan meeting to explain the situation. I went to a meeting with my assistant and was impressed by how orderly it was. I addressed the membership and told them that there was no need for partisans in our community, and if they couldn't behave like the rest of our people, I would take drastic measures to disband their organization. I would not tolerate crime. I said that they weren't fighting the Nazis anymore – there were only poor survivors in our community. All the partisan members promised to behave and help us stop the criminal acts.

Barely a week later, I received another report of a hold-up in the community and this time, a few people had sustained injuries. We found out, again, that two members of the partisan organization in our community were the main suspects, and this time we were pretty sure we knew who they were. I had to put a stop to it. We arrested one man and he confessed to the crimes. His father came crying to my office and tried to convince me to let his son go. I offered them a deal. I told the father that I would drop the charges if his son agreed to be sent to a DP camp in Germany and never come back to Bindermichl. If the father wanted to see his son, he would have to go to Germany – they could never meet again in our community. Both the father and son agreed and signed a contract with the police department to that effect. A member of our community – Abraham from the Bricha organization – took the son to one of the DP camps in Germany. We didn't like moving someone out of the community – he had to leave his family behind and I knew the whole family well – but it had to be done for the safety of our people.

In July 1946, I received a visit from some oss intelligence agents who wanted me to give them the names of the leaders of the Bricha and the Irgun in Bindermichl. The US intelligence organization was trying to stop Jewish survivors from going to pre-state Israel, then British Mandate Palestine. I refused to give them the names. I had a major conflict with the oss over the illegal movement of Jews to pre-state Israel from Bindermichl. The oss agents had already given me a lot of warnings about immigration activities in our community that they didn't like, but I didn't care. They didn't have to like it. After what our survivors had suffered in the Holocaust, I gladly helped the Bricha and the Irgun accomplish their agendas.

When the US agents asked me for the names of the leaders of the Bricha and the Irgun, I told the US agents – through an interpreter – that my police department's job was to keep law and order in our community. I didn't have a political police department and it wasn't my job to watch over political organizations. The agents asked the question again, and I again gave the same answer. Then I got angry. I told the US agents that even if I had known the names, I wouldn't give them up. I was a Holocaust survivor. I had suffered terribly and lost all my loved ones. I had gotten myself back on my feet and regained some pride and dignity. I was the proud chief of the Jewish police department in Linz-Bindermichl. I was furious with the US agents. I said that during the Holocaust the Nazis and the rest of the world had robbed me of my dignity – now that I had it back, I would hold onto it forever.

The agents looked at each other and then asked me the same question again. I still refused to give them the names of men whom I considered to be Jewish heroes. I knew the names very well – we were even friends. The US agents actually knew the names – and the addresses – of the people that they wanted from me as well. I have no idea why they wanted me to give them the names. The agents also wanted me to give them a police officer to take them to the leaders' homes. Again I refused.

As a consequence of this encounter, the oss agents arrested me right there in my office. I was charged with not cooperating with them and with helping to hide Jewish leaders who were organizing illegal transports of Jews to pre-state Israel. I was also charged with tolerating the operation of the black market in my community. To make matters worse, I was arrested three days before my wedding to Eva.

My police officers wanted to block the exit from the police station so that the OSS agents couldn't get me out of the building, but I told them to let it go. I didn't want to involve them. Looking back, I'm sorry that I let the American agents take me to jail. My men were right – they couldn't arrest me without a special court order. I was put into jail in my police uniform. I was shocked and disappointed at this turn of events.

It took some work from UNRRA Director McLynn, Chaplain Goldenberg, the president of the Jewish committee of Linz, Mr. Friedman, my good friend Ted Ciekanski and other important people, but after a few hours I was free. I was escorted back to my office and the OSS agents came to apologize for arresting me.

Another time, a high-ranking US military officer in charge of fighting crime and black markets in Linz and the surrounding districts came to my office accompanied by the chief of the Austrian criminal police, a CID officer and a sergeant in the military police who spoke Yiddish to me. They said that there was still a black market for dollars, cigarettes and other items operating in our community of Bindermichl. I got a little angry at the US officer in charge. Although there was some misbehaviour and small-time illegal activity in our community, we had no real crime. So, again through the interpreter, I respectfully said that the accusation was false. I asked my visitors how many of the survivors were in their jails for black marketeering. If people from Bindermichl were guilty of criminal activity, I said, then the US and Austrian authorities wouldn't be shy about putting our people in jail. The high-ranking US officer apologized for the accusation and asked me to continue my good work. Then they left my office.

My job as the chief of the Jewish police department in our DP community of Linz-Bindermichl was important to me. I was honoured to wear the uniform of a Jewish police officer with the Star of David – not the yellow star of shame and humiliation. The Austrian police, people and authorities gave me their full respect and attention. I was once again a proud Jew.

Time to Leave

Eva and I got married in Salzburg, Austria on July 16, 1946 – a joyous day. Our wedding ceremony was performed by an Orthodox rabbi, with all the Jewish traditions, in a hall at the large Dietlman Gasthof restaurant at Ignaz Harrer-Strasse 13. Our good friends Reina and Henry Springer, whom we had met not long after liberation, turned our wedding into a double celebration – they had a Pidyon HaBen, a traditional Jewish ceremony to recognize a family's firstborn male child, for their son, Felix, when he was four weeks old.[1]

A lot of our close friends attended our wedding, including representatives from the Jewish police and the Jewish committee in Linz-Bindermichl, Chaplain Goldenberg, two Catholic chaplains, some CID officers and other friends from Salzburg. But there was no one from either my family or Eva's family to celebrate our simcha (festive occasion). We were the only survivors from our two large families. The absence of our families cast a dark shadow over us. It was so painful not to have our loved ones with us to celebrate and share in our happiness. We never forget our loved ones – even on happy occasions.

In 1947, I went to Dachau in Germany with a small group of survi-

---

1 For more on Pidyon HaBen, see the glossary.

vors to testify in the US court proceedings against Nazi SS guards who had worked at KZ Gusen II.[2] I was accompanied by Leon Smolarz, Leon Green, Markus Grüber and Bernard Goldstein. We had a difficult time getting from Austria to Germany – transportation was still slow and complicated after the war – but nothing would deter us from testifying publicly as state witnesses so the whole world would know how the Nazis had murdered Jews.

When we arrived in Dachau, we visited the US army's Detachment 7708, War Crimes Group and met US civilian and military officials. Most of them were lawyers, prosecutors, MPs and CIC agents. We couldn't get too close to the Nazis – they were guarded closely by Polish soldiers in black uniforms. The guards told us that they were under strict orders to protect the evil Nazis from harm – especially from Jewish survivors. I wasn't too pleased to hear that, but I was only a survivor, and I didn't have any say in the matter. Even the Polish guards weren't pleased with having to protect the Nazi murderers. I was very disappointed in those circumstances.

We all went into the military Court of Justice and saw the faces of the Nazis who were on trial. They were smiling and really enjoying themselves. When we, as survivors, asked them questions or reminded them about the terrible crimes they had committed in the camp against innocent, unarmed human beings, they laughed and joked as if they were at a Nazi party. They laughed in our faces. It was a shame to watch how the Nazi murderers behaved in a court of justice. Even when the US attorneys asked them questions, the Nazi murderers laughed at them. Whenever they did answer, they made jokes or said they didn't remember and smiled. The Nazis weren't at all serious about answering for their crimes against humanity. They

---

2 The Mauthausen-Gusen trials were organized through the Dachau International Military Tribunal. Two sets of trials took place – in March 1946 and August 1947 – in which sixty-nine camp commandants, kapos and other camp administrators were charged with war crimes.

were too sure that they wouldn't be punished.[3] To them, the process was a big joke. It looked that way to me too – the Court of Justice against Nazi war criminals looked like a circus. We had survived the Holocaust. Our innocent families had been destroyed by the Nazis. And we were being humiliated again by the same Nazi murderers? We all decided to go back to Linz-Bindermichl.

I went to the US attorney in charge and told him how we felt. He was Jewish, so I was able to speak to him in Yiddish. We'd been surprised to see such injustice in an American court and we were very disappointed in the proceedings. I told him that we refused to take any more humiliation from the Nazis and that we wouldn't stay there any longer. The attorney told me that I was right – the Nazis' behaviour in court was disgusting. He prepared the papers we needed to return home.

For me, that experience in Dachau was a big shock. I had brought survivors to the military court in Dachau to testify against the ruthless Nazis – to tell how they had murdered our people and committed crimes against humanity. But we didn't get a chance to tell the military court about their brutality. Instead, we had been humiliated by the Nazi bandits, as we had been humiliated when they were still our guards in Mauthausen and Gusen. I felt as though I was back in Gusen II and that the Nazis were my superiors again. It was hard for me to understand why we had even been asked to go to Dachau to be witnesses against the Nazi murderers.

After those events in Dachau, Eva and I were anxious to get out of Austria and Europe. We had terrible memories of Mauthausen, Gusen II and Gunskirchen. We had suffered too much in Austria to be able to stay – the pain just wouldn't go away. It would be with us forever. Austria was no place for a survivor. We had no desire to build our future there.

---

3 Most of the defendants in the Mauthausen-Gusen trials were sentenced to death by hanging and the rest were sentenced to life imprisonment.

I had family in Johannesburg, South Africa – my aunt, my father's sister, and her four daughters – but I knew only their names and what city they lived in. I hoped to find my relatives in Johannesburg – perhaps my wife and I could immigrate there to be close to the small family that I had left. So I wrote a letter to the Johannesburg police and city hall, but they couldn't find my family. I think the South African officials didn't even try to find them, so immigrating to South Africa didn't work out for us.

As it happens, I did find this part of my family in 1949, when the Jewish Immigrant Aid Society (JIAS) in Montreal found my Johannesburg relatives.[4] I was so glad to finally get their contact information and I'm still in regular communication with my family there, especially with my cousin Becky. My cousin Becky's daughter, Marcelle, a beautiful young woman, came to Montreal in 2006 and I was so pleased to meet her; it was wonderful to spend time with some of my family. She is very special to us. After a year, she went back to Johannesburg and married a fine man. They have two sons and one daughter, Ilana, who once came to Miami at the same time we were there, with her girlfriend and her parents. I was fortunate to meet Ilana, and my cousin from Montreal, Joe Wolman, met her too.

But this came much later – while I was still in Bindermichl, neither Eva nor I knew of any living relatives who could help us emigrate from Austria. We would have to find another way to leave that place, with all its memories of mass murder. At the time, I had no choice but to wait for an opportunity.

Our chance came in the spring of 1948. I was in my office when I received a telephone call from our good friend Bobby Zolna, who told me that she had made an appointment for me at the Canadian

---

4 The Jewish Immigrant Aid Society (JIAS) was the most active organization providing help to Jewish refugees in Canada after World War II. For more information, see the glossary.

consulate to register for a visa to Canada. Eva and I were excited about this news, even though I didn't know anything about Canada at the time. I didn't even know where it was, let alone what kind of life we could expect there. I didn't know if there were any Jews there. But I didn't care. I wanted to get out of Austria as fast as possible.

Bobby Zolna had good connections at the Canadian consulate. Her father was the president of the Jewish committee in Linz and knew a lot of influential people at the consulate, so I felt that we had a good chance of being able to go to Canada. I was grateful to Bobby for making such an important appointment. She gave me a lot of hope.

When I visited the Canadian consulate, the consul was very friendly, which gave me a positive feeling about applying to immigrate to Canada. Once we'd made the decision, waiting to hear whether we'd been accepted was very nerve-wracking. A few weeks after that first appointment, I got a call to go to take a furrier's exam from the fur commission that had arrived from Toronto, Canada.[5] I had no idea that I was going to have to take this exam, but decided to take it anyway. The exam was being held in a large building and when I got there, a lot of furriers were already waiting outside. Some were furriers by trade and most of the people there knew at least something about the trade. I, on the other hand, wasn't a furrier and didn't know anything about the trade. I regretted my decision to go.

I was called into a large room where I met the commission of about five Jewish furriers from Toronto. I was very relieved when

---

5 In 1947, the Fur Trade Association of Canada lobbied the Department of Labour and Immigration Branch of the Canadian government, arguing that their industry was facing an extreme labour shortage. The government gave approval for five hundred skilled workers to be brought into the country (though much less of those spots were actually filled), and a "fur workers selection team" left Canada for the DP camps of Europe in the spring of 1948 to recruit potential immigrants. See Irving Abella and Harold Troper, *None Is Too Many: Canada and the Jews of Europe, 1933–1948* (Toronto: Key Porter, 2008).

they spoke to me in Yiddish. They asked me my name and whether I was an experienced furrier. I told them that I wasn't a furrier at all and didn't want to write the exam – I didn't want to waste their time – but if they could take me to Canada I would be very grateful. I said that I had no other place to go and I just couldn't remain in Austria any longer. The Toronto furriers looked at each other and then went into another room. After a short time, they came back to me and said that I was an honest man. I had told them the truth – that I wasn't a furrier – and they had decided that my application to immigrate would be accepted. They asked me if I had a trade. When I said yes – that I was a skilled housepainter – they said that I'd manage just fine in Canada. That was the best news I'd heard all day!

I was thrilled and so was Eva. We had to go for a medical exam and after that it wasn't too long before we got a call telling us to go to Port Bremerhaven in Germany. We went to a transit camp there and, while waiting for the ship, we saw a lot of people from our DP community in Linz-Bindermichl. We were all anxiously waiting to go to Canada, even though we didn't know anything about it. We were excited to be leaving the place that held so many bitter memories. We hoped for a better future for all of us in a new country.

On a happy day in October 1948, Eva and I made the big move to Canada. We left the transit camp in Bremerhaven and boarded a small military transport ship called the USS *General M.B. Stewart*. As the ship started to leave the port for the open ocean, we knew that we were leaving Europe behind for good.

The next day, we ran into a terrible storm. The sky and ocean were black. Our ship seemed out of control – at times the mast was close to the water. We were all terrified, especially because this was our first ocean voyage. We were afraid that we wouldn't make it to Canada, but we pushed away our fears. Most of the passengers were seasick. Eva was sick until we arrived in Halifax, Canada. Fortunately, the ship's captain and his crew were very kind to us; we were all grateful for their help.

I didn't have any problems with seasickness. In fact, I worked on the ship as a police officer. Although the journey wasn't pleasant, we had survived worse storms during the Holocaust. I was content to be on that small boat because I knew that we would soon be in Canada. I was anxious to get settled in my new home. Not knowing the language was a little scary, but I spoke Yiddish and I was feeling optimistic. After a week at sea, we came into the port of Halifax, ready to face the future in our new country.

When our ship docked in Halifax, it was the eve of the Jewish New Year – Rosh Hashanah – and some people from the local Jewish community came aboard to ask if we would like to stay in the city over the high holidays so we wouldn't have to travel by train to Montreal during the holiday.[6] Some of our people, including my wife and I, decided to accept that generous invitation. The Jewish people in Halifax were very friendly and spoke to us in Yiddish, so we felt at home. They took all of us from the port to a nice hotel.

The next day was Rosh Hashanah. In the morning, a Jewish man from the Halifax community came to our hotel to tell us that he would take us to a synagogue for the holiday services. We got into cars that were waiting outside the hotel and drove to a modern synagogue. The service was a little different from the services in our former country, but it was nice and the cantor was very good.[7] Rosh Hashanah in Halifax was the first real holiday we'd had since we had been separated from our loved ones in 1942. The holiday was also special because it was our first Rosh Hashanah in Canada.

After the service, we were taken to visit Jewish families in Halifax. Our group – the Shnitzer family and my wife and I – visited the home of the Zemel family. The Zemels gave us a warm welcome and we

---

6 Rosh Hashanah is the holiday that marks the beginning of the Jewish year and ushers in the high holidays. For more information, see the glossary.

7 In Judaism, a cantor, also known as a *chazzan*, leads the congregation in prayer.

felt at home with them. They were very friendly. Because Eva and I hadn't been to a Jewish family holiday for so many years, we felt that we were members of their family. Mrs. Zemel placed all of us at a large table in the dining room. Eva stood up at her place and asked Mrs. Zemel if she could be of any help. Mrs. Zemel and all her guests were pleasantly surprised. Mrs. Zemel took Eva into the kitchen and they came out with delicious, traditional food prepared especially for Rosh Hashanah. I was so very proud of Eva – she was a great help to Mrs. Zemel and was appreciated by our hosts and their guests.

Eva and I were glad that we had stayed with such warm people in Halifax, but after the lovely holiday it was time to continue on to Montreal. It was hard saying goodbye to the Zemels because we already felt so close to them. They asked us to stay in Halifax – they said that they had a small Jewish community and that we would be happy there. But our destination was a transit camp in Montreal and then Toronto, where we had been assigned to go. Eva and I will always gratefully remember the warm welcome we got from the Zemel family and the whole Jewish community in Halifax.

We left Halifax and travelled by train to Montreal. The view from our train windows was gorgeous – we passed trees with red, gold and green colours. We were happy to see the beautiful nature of Canada. When we arrived in Montreal, we were taken to a transit camp in the downtown district of St. Paul for a few days. During that time, a woman we had known in Austria, Lola Lokaj, came by to visit us. She and her husband, Chaim, had come to Montreal the year before and she arranged for us to stay in Montreal instead of going on to Toronto. We were relieved to be at the end of our travels. Then a representative of the Jewish Immigrant Aid Society took me and my wife to our first home in Canada.

We moved into the home of Mrs. Weisman and her two daughters on Napoleon Street. We rented one room and had permission to use the kitchen and the bathroom. JIAS paid for our first month's rent and gave me a cheque for fifteen dollars for our first week of food. We very much appreciated their help because we didn't have any money nor anybody else to help with food and rent. After one week, I was told to go to the JIAS office on de l'Esplanade Street, but when I arrived and the people there offered me another cheque for fifteen dollars, I refused to take it. I told them that although I appreciated their help, I liked to work for my money. I needed a job. They asked me if I had a trade. I told them that I was a housepainter and the people in the office started talking to each other in English. Then one of them asked me in Yiddish if I was an experienced painter. I said yes, so he said that he had a job for me.

JIAS sent me to see a Mr. Fortus on Clark Street. He was a nice older man who, fortunately, spoke to me in Yiddish. He asked me a few questions about my trade and liked my answers, so he told me to go back to JIAS and report for work the next morning. When I went back to the JIAS, I was offered another cheque, but again I refused to take it. I told the people there that I now had a job and thanked them for their great help. But they explained that I wouldn't get my first pay cheque until a week later and that I would need money for food and streetcar tickets to go to work. I understood that they were only trying to help, so I took the cheque. I appreciated their goodwill.

The next morning, I went to work for Mr. Fortus. He didn't work himself; he had other men working for him and they spoke only French. Because I didn't speak French or English, I couldn't communicate with them while we worked. But I was lucky – my co-workers liked me from the start and they tried to help me any way they could. I got my first pay cheque after a week of work. My wage was $1.00 an hour and I was satisfied with my pay, but my co-workers came screaming to me in French. I didn't understand why they were so upset until a Jewish man who spoke Yiddish explained to me that I should be getting $1.15 an hour like the rest of the painters. They said that I was a better painter than they were, and that I should speak to Mr. Fortus about it.

When I told my new boss that my co-workers had said that I

was being underpaid and that I should get the full hourly wage, Mr. Fortus explained that I was a "greener" (a newcomer) so I got a little less money per hour. He said that when greeners went to work in any trade, they were traditionally "used out," by which he meant we were taken advantage of. Even the best workers in the trade got a little less money per hour. Mr. Fortus said that winter was coming and there wouldn't be as much work in the painting trade anyway. He also said that if I worked for another contractor, my pay would be even lower.

The painting season ended and it was true that there wasn't much work, so all of Mr. Fortus' workers were laid off. They collected unemployment insurance and I was left to finish one last job. Then I had to look for other work. That was too bad. I had enjoyed working for Mr. Fortus, despite receiving less pay than my co-workers.

Luckily, Eva got a job as a finisher at the Taran Fur Company, where she earned $18.00 a week. JIAS took $2.00 from her pay for the train ride from Halifax to Montreal, so her real pay was only $16.00. But we managed well. We were glad that we were able to pay back the money to JIAS.

When we travelled to Montreal from Halifax, our baggage went on to Winnipeg by mistake. The transport company had sent our baggage to people named Stermer, not Sterner, so all our winter clothing was in Winnipeg. Eva and I had no choice but to buy new winter clothing in Montreal. Because of the harsh winters there, we had to be well dressed to keep warm. We couldn't afford to get sick – we had to work and we had to wait outside in the cold for streetcars to go to work. We finally got back our winter clothing – very old clothing – a few months later.

Two months after I was laid off by Mr. Fortus, I was fortunate to get a job at the largest painting company owned by Jews in Montreal – Charney Brothers on Marianne Street East. My new boss, Mr. Hy Charney, was a charming and friendly man. There were a lot of other greeners on the job, but we did the best quality work and worked in the homes of some of the most prominent people in Montreal.

We worked in Hampstead, Westmount and the Town of Mont Royal (TMR). I was happy to work for this company because I enjoyed doing quality work.

But I was underpaid there too, even though I was in charge of men on the job. Mr. Fortus had been right when he said that I would be paid even less in another place. It was a tradition to use out the greeners and I was still a greener. I liked my new boss, but he only paid me eighty-five cents an hour. According to the construction union and the Joint Committee, part of the local building trades council in Montreal, painters – qualified or unqualified – were legally entitled to $1.15 an hour. I was badly underpaid for a long time, but I had to stay because I needed the income. On the one hand, I was unhappy being so underpaid because Mr. Charney knew that I was more skilled at my trade than most of his other painters. On the other hand, I still remembered where I came from and how much more I had now. In Montreal, I had freedom, a roof over my head and a clean place to live. I wasn't hungry. When I thought about life during the Holocaust, I knew that my dear wife and I were so much better off now. Even with a little less pay, we were doing very well. The problem was that I trusted my boss. He told me that I'd get my full hourly wage of $1.15 very soon, but soon never came. I eventually gave up and went to the office to ask for my unemployment book. The office secretary, Sylvie, said that I would have to speak to Mr. Charney, so I did. I gave him ten days' notice and said that I'd be out for good. I was sorry, but I had no other choice and hoped for the best.

The next day, Ben Charney came to my job site. He was Mr. Charney's nephew and one of the managers. He said that he was surprised to learn about my problem. He was sure that I had been getting a higher wage than the other painters because he was aware how much I knew about painting. I was also in charge of important jobs. I had not only painted homes but also decorated synagogues and theatres. Ben said that something was clearly wrong. He asked me to stay on the job and said that he would see to it that I got what I was entitled to.

A week later, my pay was increased to $1.00 an hour. I was still very unhappy, but after a few more weeks I finally received an hourly wage of $1.15. I was still angry because I'd been used, however, even though I also felt that it was my own fault for not standing up for myself earlier. I hadn't been aggressive enough about getting my full hourly wage. I should have threatened to quit the job months earlier.

During that winter, Eva and I registered at Baron Byng High School on St. Urbain Street for English lessons. We went to classes two nights a week from eight to ten. We needed to learn English to communicate with people in Canada, but after six weeks at night school – which I liked very much – I had to stop my lessons because I was asked to work a night shift painting at Pesner Brothers, a large supermarket. Dropping out of my English lessons was a huge mistake. I should have told my boss that I was attending night classes for English and I should have asked him to put me on the day shift. But at the time, I didn't know him very well and, because I was still a greener, I was afraid of losing my job. I thought that I had no choice but to stop night school for the winter season. I thought that I would start English lessons again the next year, but I never ended up going back.

In 1950, Eva and I decided to move to Toronto so I could work for another contractor and find out what kind of work was being done there. I wanted to find out if Toronto and Montreal were different. I also wanted to work with my friend Manny Olmer, a painting contractor who was originally from Krakow and who now lived in Toronto.

I got a job at Miller's painting company. Mr. Miller was an older Jewish man and he liked me. I got better pay in Toronto than I had in Montreal and, after only a week, Mr. Miller asked me to take over the foreman's job in his company of eighteen painters. He also promised to give me a new panel truck. But I didn't like Toronto – everything was closed on Sundays and there was much less of a sense of community than there was in Montreal. I was miserable there, so I decided to go back to Montreal after only four weeks. That may have been another mistake, but we returned to Montreal where at least Eva had a good job and we had a lot of friends. I went back to work at Charney Brothers. I liked working for this company mainly because of the professional work that we did. I took a lot of pride in my trade. Mr. Charney appreciated my work and knew that he could depend on me. I was lucky to be liked by my boss and my co-workers. I was popular with all his customers as well.

I always worked in fine, private homes and a lot of my boss's customers asked me why I didn't go into business for myself. They used to tell me that, with my extensive knowledge of the trade, I would make an excellent contractor. A lot of customers encouraged me to go out on my own. But I wasn't sure enough of myself. I didn't speak any French or English yet, I didn't know many people in Montreal, and I wasn't sure about everything that was involved in contracting. I still had nightmares and awful memories, so I didn't yet feel as if I was on solid ground; I was still a little shaky. My wife tried to help me – she did all she could – but she was in the same situation. She also had horrible dreams and bad memories. We were trying to have a normal life, but after living through the Holocaust and losing our loved ones, we found it very hard.

In 1950, Mr. Charney put me in charge of three painters in a beautiful home in Upper Westmount that belonged to Mr. and Mrs. Jerry Cohen. Mr. Charney promised to mix the colours himself for the Cohens' new home. My three painters and I started to prepare for the painting job. Unfortunately, Mr. Charney wasn't very good at keeping his promises. He was never on time and on this occasion he didn't show up at all. After a few days, Mr. Cohen became really angry. He called Charney's office many times but got no results. Mr. Cohen became even more upset with Mr. Charney for ignoring his calls and said that if Charney did come, he wouldn't even let him into the house. He then asked me to mix the colours for his home so we didn't have to wait for Mr. Charney. I wasn't sure if I had the right to mix the colours after my boss had promised to mix them, so I asked, "What will Mr. Charney say?" Mr. Cohen said that I should never be afraid to make my boss's customers happy.

I felt as though I had no choice, so I started mixing the colours to match the fabrics and carpets. Fortunately, I knew my trade well. I made very close matches, and Mr. and Mrs. Cohen liked the colours very much. After I had finished with the colours, Mr. Charney walked in and greeted us all with a friendly smile. I was sure that Mr. Cohen wouldn't talk to him, but to my surprise he greeted him warmly. Returning his smile, Mr. Cohen asked my boss if he had forgotten his promise to mix the colours himself. Mr. Charney responded that he knew that Willie was in charge and he could be trusted to mix the colours well. Mr. Charney had a lot of charm, so nobody could stay angry with him. And when we finished the painting job, Mr. Cohen was pleased with our work. In the end, everyone was happy.

Later, Jerry Cohen asked me why I was working for Mr. Charney. He said that I should open my own paint contracting company and work for myself. I said that I didn't know very many people in Montreal and that I was unsure of myself because of my poor English. Mr. Cohen said that if I started my own painting company, he would pay me the difference if I earned less than what I made at Charney's place. I'd have no problem, he assured me. His lovely wife, Elenora, said that if Jerry told me to go on my own, he would keep his promise and I'd be okay. I wasn't too sure, but somehow I started to feel optimistic.

A few weeks later, I gave notice to Mr. Charney's office that I was leaving the company because I was going to start my own painting company. They didn't believe me, but I did start the Willie Sterner Painting and Decorating Company at the end of 1950. I told Jerry Cohen that I had started my own company. He offered me mazel tov (congratulations) and said that I had made a good move. He told me not to worry, that I'd be fine. Still, I was a little scared. Starting my own business was a big step. But I knew my trade well and I had the support of Jerry Cohen. I trusted him all the way. I hoped to be healthy and lucky in my new venture. I would have to work hard to make a successful company. I didn't want to disappoint Mr. Cohen.

My company's first painting contract was in Hampstead. I was fortunate that my first customers were lovely people. I did a nice painting job in their home. They were pleased with the job and with my good service and I felt more confident about my future. Mr. Cohen recommended me to customers such as Mr. and Mrs. Charles Balinsky. They were warm people and I enjoyed painting their beautiful home. From the start of my contracting, the Cohens and the Balinskys were my most prominent customers. But all my customers were lovely people. It was a pleasure to work for them, and satisfied customers recommended me to their friends.

I took pride in my work and I was paid well. I got much more than most other painters did. I was always working on jobs for my special customers. My only advertisement came from satisfied customers and the quality of my work. Unfortunately, I was a better tradesman than I was a businessman, so my profits could have been better. For me, my real profit came when I saw that my customers were pleased with the painting job. I was happy with what I was doing and I was making a decent living.

In February 1952, Eva and I were thrilled with the birth of our first son, Harry, at the Jewish General Hospital in Montreal. We named our beautiful baby after my late father, Hersz Leib Sterner, and we celebrated Harry's birth and bris at the hospital with a little party with our friends.[8] The event was a big simcha for us because we had so little family left from the Holocaust. Four weeks later, Harry had a Pidyon HaBen because he was the firstborn son. It was a pleasure and

---

8 A bris is a Jewish religious ceremony to welcome male infants into the covenant with God. It involves ritual circumcision and is performed eight days after the baby is born. For more information, see the glossary.

a simcha to watch our son playing, smiling at us and sleeping. We were a small, loving family but still sad that we had no other family members with whom we could share our happiness.

On January 26, 1956, we had another happy day when our second son, named Abraham (Abie) after my wife's father, was born. Abie was also born in the Jewish General Hospital and we had a bris for him there. Harry was excited about having a baby brother and loved him very much. Our Abie was a lovely child – active and smart. He was a self-sufficient baby, always wanting to make everything himself. He loved to play with his older brother and we loved to watch Harry take care of Abie. We were the proud parents of two lovely boys. We hoped that they would grow up with good health and good fortune. Harry and Abie were our little family's joy, pride and happiness.

Time went by quickly. Our children grew up and went to school. When Harry had his bar mitzvah at the Young Israel of Val Royal synagogue, it was one of the happiest days of our lives. He read his Haftorah very well.[9] We had a luncheon after the service and more than two hundred guests visited our synagogue. In the evening, we had a special party for our close friends and Harry's friends in our home. We still missed our loved ones.

Four years later, Abie had his bar mitzvah at the same synagogue. When the time came for Abie to say the Haftorah, with more than two hundred guests listening, Abie stood near the Torah and didn't say anything – he told us later that he couldn't remember how to say his portion. My wife got so scared! But when the rabbi calmly told Abie to recite the Haftorah he had prepared, he recited it beautifully. The rabbi also told him to finish the prayer with the Adon Olam, and

---

9 A bar mitzvah is the Jewish ritual and family celebration that marks the religious coming of age of a boy at the age of thirteen. The Haftorah is the portion of the Hebrew Bible that is read out and sung at the ceremony.

he made a good speech.[10] Just as we had with Harry, we had a party at the synagogue and another party at our home at night. The event was a lovely simcha, even though Abie had given us a good scare!

Growing up, Harry and Abie had been deprived of their grandparents – their bubby and zaida – as well as uncles, aunties and cousins. Our sons had no relatives to spoil them and give them lots of love. When they were young, they didn't understand why they didn't have a bubby and a zaida like their Canadian friends did and they wanted to know why. They felt that they were missing an important part of their family, especially on high holidays, at their bar mitzvahs and at other celebrations. It was hard for them to understand and it was painful for all of us. When Harry later became the father of two lovely girls – Jessica and Melanie – he told them to enjoy their bubby and zaida because he hadn't had the pleasure and the privilege of having grandparents to love and spoil him.

~

At work, my painters and I served our customers for many years. I didn't push my painters to work fast and they were paid more than the legal wage. They had steady jobs and I was pleased with their performance. But after a number of years in business, I started to have problems with some of my men. They became insubordinate – they started to come to work late and their work started to get sloppy. Their behaviour reflected badly on my company. I felt betrayed by my men and I couldn't understand the change.

I had always provided excellent service to my customers, but now I was at a loss as to what to do. I tried to explain to my men that I had a responsibility to my customers and that I wanted them to go back to

---

10 The Adon Olam (in Hebrew, literally, "Lord of the World") is a hymn about God's presence and empowerment that is traditionally sung at the closing of synagogue services, both on the Sabbath and to mark the end of major festivals.

behaving professionally on the job. They answered that if I didn't like their work, I should give them their unemployment insurance books. I had only two reliable painters – Stefan Longo and Nick Andreculac – and I was in the middle of painting jobs. It was a terrible situation.

I got so fed up with my problems that I decided to try working with a partner and went into a partnership with a Jewish painting contractor named Joe Goldberg. I told Joe that we should go into commercial painting, but he wasn't as interested in that, so I told him that I wanted to get out of the painting trade and look for a different kind of small business. As much I loved my trade, I now felt that I had had enough – there was too much aggravation. I wanted something that I could work at alone. Joe didn't believe that I would ever leave the painting business, but I did get out eventually, and we parted on friendly terms.

I didn't have much money and I wasn't that young anymore. The only trade I knew was the painting trade. Despite all of this, I decided to try out a new business. In July 1978, I leased a little tobacco store in an office building at 2050 Mansfield Street. The store had closed because the previous tenants couldn't pay the rent, but it was nicely equipped and air-conditioned. When I started my new venture, I didn't know anything about running a store. I didn't smoke anymore, so I didn't know anything about the cigarette brands or package sizes. But I grew to like my small store. It was a pleasant place to work and the customers were friendly.

The work was hard at the beginning, but I didn't care. My first four months were not at all profitable – I had to pay the rent out of my own pocket. I was lucky that my wife had a job at the factory – the second income gave me the opportunity to build my business. Any small profit that I made, I used to increase the stock. My landlord asked me how I would be able to pay the rent. My accountant asked the same question, but he wished me good luck. I did worry and I did struggle, but I didn't give up hope. I worked hard. For five days a week, I worked in my store by myself from six o'clock in the morning to six in the evening. I really wanted to make the venture work.

Over the first couple of months, I started making changes. When I got the store, it was a little tobacco store. I turned it into a little restaurant and grocery store. I sold beer, wine, pizza, sandwiches, coffee, bagels and cakes. I sold office supplies, pharmaceutical articles, Loto-Québec tickets and much more. My business started to get better and better every day. After four months, I finally started to take home a small profit. I liked working in my store so much more than painting. I would never go back to painting even if I were offered double what I made in the store.

After three years of working by myself, I got so busy that I had to ask Eva to leave her job and help me in the store. She was glad to work with me. She was friendly to our customers and they liked her very much. My wife was a great help, a real partner in the business. I had become an experienced storekeeper myself, and we made a good living.

After six-and-a-half years, however, I had a little misunderstanding with my landlord, so I had to sell the store. I regret what happened and I realized later that I was at fault. What happened was that when I had only one year left in my lease, I happened to mention in passing that I was thinking of selling the store. My landlord liked me very much and we had become friends. When I said that to him, that I was thinking of selling the store, he responded by saying that he hoped that he would be lucky enough to find a new tenant who was like me. I got upset that he didn't talk me out of selling, and I didn't react rationally. Even though my landlord tried to calm me down by suggesting that I could stay on, my stupid pride took over and I chose to sell my store. What a terrible mistake!

Meanwhile, Harry had married a lovely young woman named Silvia in 1980 and they had given us two lovely granddaughters, Jessica Rose and Melanie. Jessica was born on February 25, 1981, and Melanie was born two years later, on July 6, 1983. Our grandchildren have given us so much joy. Every Friday while they were young, the two girls slept at our home. We had Sabbath meals with them and they lit the Sabbath candles in the Jewish tradition. On Saturdays, we spent time with them at the park or took them to shopping malls. Jessica and Melanie were well behaved and loved to stay with their bubby and zaida – we loved having them with us for the Sabbath.

Jessica Rose and Melanie had their bat mitzvahs at the Lubavitch organization.[11] It was so lovely when they recited their small portions from the bat mitzvah book! We served lunch and had a party after the ceremony; it was a wonderful simcha. Our families and friends were there to celebrate. We were proud of our granddaughters. The girls danced and sang well into the evening.

On July 23, 1983, Abie married a lovely young woman named Nicole who already had a baby girl named Patricia who was less than one year old. Abie adopted Patricia so she became a Sterner, and we were delighted to have her officially become our granddaughter. Then on March 26, 1990, Abie and Nicole became the parents of a beautiful girl named Seana – she was smart and self-sufficient, just like her father was at her age. She was so energetic, always on the move. Seana was a joy to her parents and to her bubby and zaida.

Eva and I thank God that we became the parents and grandparents of such a lovely family. We hope that our family will always be healthy and successful – they give us hope and pride. My two sons work hard – Harry is the manager at a meat-packing company and Abie is a partner in a high-tech firm – and their fine wives help create a wonderful family life. Our children and grandchildren come to our home every Friday for Shabbat dinner. We have lots of fun when the whole family is together. For survivors like Eva and me, staying close to family is the best possible medicine. We hope our family happiness will last for a very long time.

---

11 The Lubavitch movement is a branch of Orthodox, Hasidic Judaism. For more information, see the glossary.

Speaking Out

On May 25, 1984, one of our dreams came true – Eva and I went to Israel for the first time. We went with a group from Toronto for only four short weeks. We met people from Canada, the United States, Australia, South Africa, Germany and other places. We also saw people we hadn't seen for a long time. We had such a lovely time – a time to remember.

My wife and I were impressed with Israel's achievements. The country was beautiful, democratic and very modern. The people were proud and friendly. We saw the most important places in Israel and I was proud to see our Jewish soldiers and the Jewish police. We also visited the Israeli Knesset (parliament). We were glad that we could visit Israel and we hoped to go again soon with the whole family.

I was only sorry that my father's dream of going to Israel never materialized. He was a real Zionist and a strong believer in the Jewish State of Israel. Before the war, my father had told us that he planned to move us to pre-state Israel, but the Nazis took away his chance – our whole family's chance – to settle in Israel all those years ago.

When I retired in 1986, Eva and I began to divide our time between Montreal and Miami Beach, Florida, where we went in the winter. I used to love the winters in Canada when I was younger, but we weren't young anymore and it had gotten harder and harder to take the snow, ice and bitter cold of the Canadian winter. It was also dangerous – we could fall down on the ice and break our bones. But Eva and I do enjoy winters in Miami.

I decided that it was time for me to speak out, to warn people about the dangers of hate and prejudice. In Miami Beach, I got involved with the Holocaust Documentation and Education Center. Through the Montreal Holocaust Memorial Centre, I also started going on speaking tours. I went to high schools, universities, colleges, synagogues, churches, retirement homes and condos. Although I found it painful to speak about the Holocaust, I felt that it was my duty to speak for those who cannot speak any more.

My decision to speak out and work with Holocaust centres coincided with the release of the movie *Schindler's List* in 1993. We were in Miami at the time, and Jessica and Melanie had come to visit us from Montreal and they wanted to see the movie. They knew that I had worked at Schindler's Emalia, but Eva and I were afraid to take them to see the movie because they were too young. Jessica was twelve years old and Melanie was ten. They pleaded with me – their zaida – to take them to the movie. I felt I had no choice – we went to see *Schindler's List*. When the movie started, I couldn't watch the scene in the Krakow ghetto because my father and two younger brothers were murdered there. But I was glad that we had seen *Schindler's List* together because our granddaughters understood something about our suffering and the loss of our loved ones in the Holocaust.

The executive director of the Holocaust Center in Miami Beach was Mrs. Rosita Ehrlich Kenigsberg, whom I had known in Montreal when she was a small child. Rosita knew that I had worked for Oskar Schindler because I had spoken about Schindler's Emalia with her parents at their home in Montreal long before *Schindler's List* came out. So, when *Schindler's List* came to Miami and journalists were asking for interviews with survivors who had worked for Schindler, Rosita referred them to me. I was the first to be interviewed by Channel 4 and Channel 10 and by the *Miami Herald*.

In February 1994, my wife and I were invited to Detroit by the

Children of Holocaust Survivors Association of Michigan (CHAIM), an organization of sons and daughters of Holocaust survivors. It was my first public speaking appearance and I was extremely nervous. I wasn't a public speaker – I hadn't gone to English schools and my English wasn't good. But I got support from the president of CHAIM, Dr. Charles Silow. He gave me a lot of encouragement and said that I would be fine. The people at CHAIM were kind to us too. Harry and Abie came from Canada to Detroit to give me their support.

We went to the Jewish centre in West Bloomfield, a suburb of Detroit, where about seven hundred guests (Jews and non-Jews) and news reporters with TV cameras waited. Before I spoke, Dr. Charles Silow introduced me, but I was so nervous that I didn't even thank him for the introduction. Then I spoke for about an hour and a half. I described what I went through and I didn't need any papers to help me. After my speech, I answered questions from the floor for half an hour. The public gave me a standing ovation and I was asked to sign autographs. I was told that I gave a good speech, but I was glad when it was over.

On April 10, 1994, I spoke about the Holocaust and Oskar Schindler in Nashville, Tennessee. The Jewish Federation of Nashville had invited me to speak and the event took place in the private home of Jerry and Beth Tannenbaum. The house, which was located up a steep hill, was large and elegant. About eighty people were anxious to hear about my terrible experiences during the Holocaust. They appreciated my speech and my visit to Nashville.

On April 29, 1994, I went to Ottawa with Eva to speak about the Holocaust to the Young Women's Leadership Council at the Agudath Israel congregation. The people were pleased that I came to speak to them about the Holocaust, Oskar Schindler and KZ Płaszów. I was glad to be there even though the event was hard on my wife and me. When I spoke, painful reminders of my tragedy came back, but the audience was interested in learning about it.

On November 21, 1994, I visited North Dade Middle School in

Opa-Locka (Miami Beach) with some other survivors. The young students interviewed us about the Holocaust. I was interviewed by a lovely twelve-year-old girl named Barbara Zarandy. The event was emotional for all of us, but it was interesting to be interviewed by such young people. They asked important questions about our terrible tragedy. I was glad to be there and I will always remember that day.

I became very active in talking to even more groups about fighting hate and prejudice. I aimed to enlighten students in high schools, universities and colleges about the Holocaust. I explained to young people how six million innocent Jews perished, how they were brutally murdered and how the whole world was silent. About 80 per cent of the students I have spoken to didn't know anything at all about the Holocaust. They hadn't learned about it in their homes or even in their schools. But they listened and were anxious to learn and asked important questions. They wanted to know, for example, why no one helped or defended our people. Fortunately, the young students promised to teach their families and friends about hate and the Holocaust, so I felt optimistic about my work with them and felt some hope for a better future.

On February 19, 1995, four to five thousand survivors visited the Fontainebleau Hotel in Miami Beach to mark fifty years of life after the Holocaust. Survivors came from all over the world and Eva and I were among them. Important speakers talked about our tragedy, a cantor recited Kaddish for our *keddoshim*, and we all followed along.[1] A US army band played Jewish songs and US soldiers marched onto a stage with US flags. Each flag represented a concentration camp. When a young, non-Jewish woman from the US army sang beau-

---

1 Also known as the Mourner's Prayer, Kaddish is said as part of mourning rituals in Jewish prayer services as well as at funerals and memorials. *Keddoshim* is Hebrew for "holy ones" and is also used to refer to the victims of the Holocaust. For more information on *keddoshim*, see the glossary.

tiful Jewish songs, her singing really affected us. The emotion was high and our hearts were full. My wife and I were glad that we had attended. We saw survivors and friends from the United States and Canada. I was sorry to see that not many survivors were left, but the gathering and the ceremony were impressive. We had time to properly commemorate our survival of the Holocaust and the fifty years that followed our liberation from that hell.

Five years later, the Central Agency for Jewish Education in Miami Beach sent Eva and me on a trip to Poland and Israel as part of the March of the Living.[2] On April 29, 2000, we flew from Miami to Warsaw on an El Al airplane with a large group of teenagers and staff and survivors. Our role was to enlighten our young students about what we went through in the Holocaust. My wife and I got very close to the teenagers. We took care of them and were like grandparents to them.

Yom HaShoah, Holocaust Memorial Day, occurred while we were in Poland on the March of the Living. We all wore blue jackets with the symbol of the March of the Living as we marched in silence to remember our *keddoshim*. It was an impressive sight to see thousands of Jewish people wearing blue jackets with the Star of David. In Birkenau, important speakers – including President Weizman of Israel, President Kwaśniewski of Poland and Rabbi Lau of Israel – spoke at a large and impressive ceremony.[3] A large group of Polish survivors and Polish scouts attended. We lit candles for our loved ones and recited the Kaddish and the El-Malei Rachamim.[4] Returning to

---

2 The March of the Living brings Jewish students and young adults from around the world to Poland and Israel to learn about the Holocaust. For more information, see the glossary.

3 Auschwitz II-Birkenau was a mass-murder facility built in 1942. For more information, see the glossary.

4 El-Malei Rachamim (Hebrew) translates to "God who is full of compassion" and is the prayer recited at Jewish funerals.

one of the places of mass murder in Poland and remembering the loss of our loved ones was an emotional, painful and moving experience.

We also went to Krakow. For the first time, Eva and I visited the place where my family had been murdered by the Nazis. We visited the Jewish section of Kazimierz, the temple and all the synagogues. I went to see the place in Podgórze where I had lived with my happy family until the Holocaust tore us apart. I also went with my group to Płaszów where I had worked as a slave – a visit to Płaszów hadn't been part of our plan, but I insisted that we go there. Only a monument is left in Płaszów. We recited the Kaddish.

I was disappointed to find, however, that there is nothing left of the Krakow ghetto. I lost my father and two younger brothers in an *Aktion* and thousands of other Jewish victims were murdered by the Nazis there, but now it looks as if nothing was ever there.[5] It looks as if no crime was committed there. It was a terrible blow to me. It is an injustice and a shame that our Jewish leaders have not kept the memory of the terrible tragedy in the Krakow ghetto alive. How is it that this important place is so ignored? How can we Jews forget that Jewish families lived in terror and humiliation there or that Jews were starved and murdered there? I feel that our Jewish leaders don't care. The neglect is painful for me and all Jews from Krakow. As a survivor, I am ashamed.

I was also disappointed to find that Oskar Schindler's old Emalia in Krakow was closed to the public.[6] Schindler's place should be open to the public to show the world how hard he worked to save Jews and how he risked his freedom and life to do it. This place should be a shrine – it's important that our people really understand the heroic nature of what he did for us.

---

5   In 2005, a memorial to the ghetto was erected in Plac Bohaterów Getta, or Ghetto Heroes' Square.

6   A museum that focuses on the Nazi occupation of Krakow during World War II and Oskar Schindler's role in saving Jews opened in the former administrative building of Schindler's Emalia factory on June 11, 2010.

We visited other important Jewish places, concentration camps and crematoria in Poland. We visited Lublin, Auschwitz, Majdanek, Treblinka and Tikocim, an old synagogue. Although it was painful for Eva and me, we were happy because we met our dear granddaughter Melanie in Poland. She had come with a Canadian group from Montreal. It was so helpful to have our granddaughter near us for love and support.

After a week in Poland, we left for Israel to participate in Israel Memorial Day (Yom Hazikaron). I was impressed with how the Israelis began the day – at eleven o'clock in the morning sirens blared for two minutes all over Israel and everything in Israel stood still. All the traffic stopped to pay homage to all the Israelis who have fallen in defence of the country. Later, we went to a concert at the Hordos Arena in Caesarea to celebrate the fifty-second anniversary of the birth of Israel. Among the thousands of people at the night party, we met our Melanie again in the dark. She found us! Having her with us to celebrate the anniversary made it that much more significant and moving. Eva and I were both glad that we had made the trip – it was an experience that we will never forget.

Yizkor

In memory of the many relatives I lost in the Holocaust 1939–1945.

My father, Hersz Leib Sterner, who was murdered in the Krakow
   ghetto.
My mother, Hinda Reizel Sterner, who was murdered in Treblinka.
My brother Josel Meier, who was murdered in the Krakow ghetto.
My brother Abraham, who was murdered in the Krakow ghetto.
My sister Ida, who was murdered in Treblinka.
My sister Genia, who was murdered in Treblinka.
My sister Rachel, who was murdered in Treblinka.
My sister Sarah, who was murdered in Treblinka.

From my father's side:

My dear grandmother, Miriam Brindel Sterner.
Uncle Moishe, my father's older brother, and his family – only one
   member of the family of nine, Izak, survived.
Uncle Kalman, my father's younger brother, and his family – the only
   one of the family of four to survive was my cousin Cesia Wolman.
Uncle Szklarz and his family – the only survivor from his family of
   four was a son who had gone to Israel as a *chalutz* (pioneer) before
   the war.

From my mother's side:

My dear grandparents, Mendel and Rachel Matusinski – the only survivors from their family of eight were my uncle Aaron – my mother's younger brother – and my aunt Gucia.

Other family members:

From Książ Wielki near Krakow
    Uncle Meier and his family of six
    Uncle Jankel
    Uncle Frank – he and his fiancée were both murdered by the Nazis
    Aunt Pola
    Uncle Izak Matusinski.

From Miechów
    Uncle Matus – there were no survivors from his family of four.
    Uncle Idel – no one from this family of five survived.
    From the Eisen family of seven was only one survivor, Willie.
    From the Szlivovicz family there was only one survivor, my cousin
        Joe (Silver).

From Charsznica
    The Rogowskis - there were no survivors from this large family.

Glossary

Adloyada The carnival and parade held on the Jewish holiday of Purim. The word originates from the Hebrew Talmudic saying "*ad-lo yada*," which means "until we don't know." The saying refers to the revelry that is called for during the Purim festival, encouraging drunkenness until one does not know the difference between "cursed is Haman" and "blessed is Mordecai" – two central figures in the story of Purim. *See also* Purim.

Aktion (German; plural, *Aktionen*;) The brutal roundup of Jews for forced labour, forcible resettlement into ghettos, mass murder by shooting or deportation to death camps.

American Jewish Joint Distribution Committee (JDC) Also known colloquially as the "Joint." A charitable organization that provided material support for persecuted Jews in Germany and other Nazi-occupied territories and facilitated their emigration to neutral countries such as Portugal, Turkey and China. As Nazi persecution accelerated in Germany between 1933 and 1939, the JDC increased its aid to German and Austrian Jews and helped 250,000 of them escape the country by covering travel expenses and landing fees, and securing travel accommodations and visas for countries of refuge. Between 1939 and 1944, JDC officials helped close to 81,000 European Jews to find asylum in various parts of the world. Between 1944 and 1947, the JDC assisted more than 100,000 refugees living in DP camps by offering retraining programs, cultural activities and financial assistance for emigration.

antisemitism Prejudice, discrimination, persecution and/or hatred against Jewish people, institutions, culture and symbols.

Appell (German) Roll call.

Aryan A nineteenth-century anthropological term originally used to refer to the Indo-European family of languages and, by extension, the peoples who spoke them. It became a synonym for people of Nordic or Germanic descent in the theories that inspired Nazi racial ideology. "Aryan" was an official classification in Nazi racial laws to denote someone of pure Germanic blood, as opposed to "non-Aryans," such as Jews, part-Jews, Roma (Gypsies) and others of supposedly inferior racial stock.

bar mitzvah, bat mitzvah (Hebrew; literally: one to whom commandments apply) The age of thirteen when, according to Jewish tradition, boys become religiously and morally responsible for their actions and are considered adults for the purpose of synagogue ritual. A bar mitzvah is also the synagogue ceremony and family celebration that mark the attainment of this status, during which the boy is called upon to read a portion of the Torah and recite the prescribed prayers in a public prayer forum (minyan). In the latter half of the twentieth century, liberal Jews instituted an equivalent ceremony and celebration for girls – called a bat mitzvah – that takes place at the age of twelve.

Belzec A death camp that was established in 1942 in the Lublin district, Poland. Belzec was the first of three death camps built specifically for the implementation of Operation Reinhard, the German code word for the Nazi plan for the mass extermination of European Jews. Between March and December 1942, approximately 600,000 Jews were murdered in Belzec.

bet hamidrash (Hebrew; Yiddish, *beys midrash*; house of learning) A Jewish religious study centre.

Bindermichl DP camp A Displaced Persons camp located in Linz, Austria. The Bindermichl camp was a social and cultural community; it produced newspapers that were distributed in other DP camps in Austria, and it was also where the Jewish Historical Commission, which documented war crimes, was founded. This centre was later to become Simon Wiesenthal's Jewish Historical Documentation Centre.

Birkenau One of the camps that was part of the Auschwitz complex and operated as a death camp. The gas chambers that became operational in Birkenau between January and June 1942 used Zyklon B to mass murder Jews. The camp also held four crematoria, which were constructed between March and June 1943.

Bricha (Hebrew; literally: escape) Name given to the massive organized, clandestine migration of Jews from Eastern Europe and DP camps to pre-state Israel following World War II. Estimates of the number of Jews helped by Bricha range from 80,000 to 250,000.

bris (Yiddish; Hebrew, *brit milah*; literally: the covenant of circumcision) A bris is a Jewish religious ceremony performed eight days after the baby is born to welcome male infants into the covenant with God. It involves ritual circumcision, removal of the foreskin from the penis, by a *mohel*, a person trained to perform the procedure.

bubby (Yiddish; also bubba, bubbe, bubbie, bobbe, bobe) Grandmother.

Bund (Yiddish, short for Algemeyner Yidisher Arbeter Bund in Lite, Polyn un Rusland, meaning the Jewish Workers' Alliance in Lithuania, Poland and Russia) A Jewish social-democratic revolutionary movement founded in Vilnius, Lithuania in 1897 to fight for the rights of the Yiddish-speaking Jewish worker in Eastern Europe, advocate Jewish cultural autonomy in the Diaspora and champion Yiddish language and secular culture. In interwar Poland, the Bund served as one of many Jewish political organizations that also had affiliated schools, youth groups and sports clubs.

cantor Also known as a *chazzan*, a cantor leads a Jewish congregation in prayer. Because music plays such a large role in Jewish religious services, the cantor is usually professionally trained in music.

challah (Hebrew) Braided egg bread traditionally eaten on the Jewish Sabbath, Shabbat, as well as on other Jewish holidays.

cheder (Hebrew; literally: room) An Orthodox Jewish elementary school that teaches the fundamentals of Jewish religious observance and textual study, as well as the Hebrew language.

cholent (Yiddish) A traditional Jewish slow-cooked pot stew usually eaten as the main course at the festive Shabbat lunch on Saturdays after the synagogue service and on other Jewish holidays. For Jews of East European descent, the basic ingredients of *cholent* are meat, potatoes, beans and barley.

chutzpah (Hebrew; audacity) A term that describes the quality of being brazen, nervy or shameless.

CIC The US Counter-Intelligence Corps. The organization was part of the US army; its post-war operations in Austria involved countering the black market.

CID The US Criminal Investigation Division. Now known as the US Army Criminal Investigation Command, it was the section of the US army that dealt with criminal investigation of military personnel.

Deutsche Emailwaren Fabrik The enamel factory in Krakow, Poland that was taken over by Oskar Schindler in 1940. The company had entered bankruptcy when Schindler took over the lease and the previous factory manager, Abraham Bankier, became one of Schindler's most trusted advisors. The Emalia closed in 1944, when Schindler was forced to transfer his business to the town of Brünnlitz. At its height, the Emalia employed close to 1,000 Jewish workers, who were housed in a small camp on the factory grounds. Keeping the Jewish workers onsite saved them from the horrors of Płaszów, the slave labour and concentration camp that operated nearby and that officially had authority over the sub-camp at the Emalia. The former factory site now houses a small museum focused on the Nazi occupation of Krakow as well as Schindler's heroic role in saving Jews.

Displaced Persons People who find themselves homeless and stateless at the end of a war. Following World War II, millions of people, especially European Jews, found that they had no homes to return to or that it was unsafe to do so. To resolve the staggering refugee crisis that resulted, Allied authorities and the United Nations Relief and Rehabilitation Administration (UNRRA) established Displaced Persons (DP) camps to provide temporary shelter and assistance to refugees, and help them transition towards resettlement.

DP camps Facilities set up by the Allies at the end of World War II to provide shelter for the millions of people – both Jews and non-Jews – who had been displaced from their home countries as a result of the war. In October 1945 the United Nations Relief and Rehabilitation Administration (UNRRA) took responsibility for administering these camps. *See also* United Nations Relief and Rehabilitation Administration (UNRRA).

Endeks (in Polish, *Endecja*) A political party also known as the Nationalist Democrats that was led by Polish politician Roman Dmowski. Though antisemitic – the party advocated for boycotts of Jewish businesses, a redistribution of wealth from Jews to Poles and Jewish emigration from Poland – they did not advocate for radical or violent acts against Jews.

Frank, Hans (1900–1946) Nazi governor general of the occupied area in central Poland known as the *Generalgouvernement* from 1939 to 1945. He oversaw the establishment of ghettos for Jews and forced labour for Jewish and Polish civilians.

gefilte fish A dish generally made from chopped whitefish that is made into patties and boiled. It is traditionally eaten on Shabbat, Jewish holidays and other festive occasions.

Generalgouvernement The territory in central Poland that was conquered by the Germans in September 1939 but not annexed to the

Third Reich. Made up of the districts of Warsaw, Krakow, Radom and Lublin, it was deemed a special administrative area and was used as the place for the Nazis to carry out their racial plans of murdering Jews. From 1939 onward, Jews from all over German-occupied territories were transferred to this region, as were Poles expelled from their homes in the annexed Polish territories further west.

Gestapo (German) Short for Geheime Staatspolizei, the Secret State Police of Nazi Germany. The Gestapo were a brutal force that operated with very few legal constraints in dealing with the perceived enemies of the Nazi regime and were responsible for rounding up European Jews for deportation to the death camps. A number of Gestapo members also joined the Einsatzgruppen, the mobile killing squads responsible for the roundup and murder of Jews in eastern Poland and the USSR through mass shooting operations.

ghetto A confined residential area for Jews. The term originated in Venice, Italy in 1516 with a law requiring all Jews to live on a segregated, gated island known as Ghetto Nuovo. Throughout the Middle Ages in Europe, Jews were often forcibly confined to gated Jewish neighbourhoods. During the Holocaust, the Nazis forced Jews to live in crowded and unsanitary conditions in run-down districts of cities and towns. Most ghettos in Poland were enclosed by brick walls or wooden fences with barbed wire.

Göth, Amon (1908–1946) Austrian Nazi captain and commandant of the Płaszów forced labour and concentration camp. Göth was infamous for his volatile nature and brutality against Jews. He murdered and tortured thousands of Jews and was hanged for his crimes in 1946 under a ruling by the Supreme National Tribunal of Poland.

goy (Hebrew and Yiddish; literally: nation) Originally used to denote people of "other nations," the modern usage of the term references a non-Jewish person. The term "goy" can be pejorative, depending on context.

Gunskirchen A subcamp of the Mauthausen-Gusen complex that was built in December 1944 and held more than 16,000 Hungarians, hundreds of political prisoners, and, in April 1945, thousands of Jews who had been evacuated from the Mauthausen camp. The camp, located in Upper Austria, north of the town of Gunskirchen, outside the village of Edt bei Lambach, operated from December 1944 to May 1945. The camp was immensely overcrowded and unsanitary; between two hundred and three hundred inmates died each day from typhoid fever and dysentery. The camp was liberated by American troops on May 4, 1945.

Gusen II One of the fifty subcamps in the Mauthausen-Gusen complex, the camp was founded in March 1944 – after Allied bombs had bombed the Messerschmitt aircraft factory in southern Germany – to house an underground war production plant. By September 1944, the camp held close to 20,000 prisoners, 11,000 of whom worked in the underground factory. Inmates were used to excavate tunnels and perform other laborious tasks to construct the plant, after which they then began building fuselages for the mass production of the Me262 fighter jet. The camp was overcrowded, lacked sanitary drinking water and other basic facilities, and was known as "the hell of hells"; the lifespan of a Gusen inmate was about four months.

Haftorah The portion read from the Book of Prophets after the Torah reading at Sabbath services and major festivals; it is traditionally sung by the youth who is celebrating their bar/bat mitzvah.

Hasidism (from the Hebrew word *hasid*; literally: piety) A Jewish spiritual movement founded by Rabbi Israel ben Eliezer in eighteenth-century Poland; characterized by philosophies of mysticism and focusing on joyful prayer. It stressed piety and joyful worship over the intellectual study of the Talmud. This resulted in a new kind of leader who attracted disciples as opposed to the traditional rabbis who focused on the intellectual study of Jewish law. There are many different sects of Hasidic Judaism, but followers of Hasidism often wear dark, conservative clothes as well as a head covering to reflect modesty and show respect to God. *See also* shtreimel.

Irgun (abbreviated from Irgun Zvai Le'umi; Hebrew; National Military Organization) The Irgun (also known as the Etzel, its Hebrew acronym) was formed in 1937 after it separated from the Haganah, a military organization that was operating in British Mandate Palestine between 1920 and 1948. Due to the increasing level of violence between Arab and Jewish citizens, the Irgun, under the leadership of Revisionist Zionist Ze'ev Jabotinsky, advocated active and armed resistance (in opposition to the policy of restraint that was advocated by the Haganah) as well as the establishment of a Jewish state in Palestine. The Irgun was responsible for numerous attacks in British Mandate Palestine and was also fundamental to the illegal transport and immigration of thousands of European Jews into the state. The activities of the Irgun were controversial – some viewed them as a terrorist organization, while others applauded their efforts as freedom fighters. *See also* Jabotinsky, Ze'ev.

Jabotinsky, Ze'ev (1880–1940) Ze'ev Jabotinsky was founder of the Revisionist Zionist movement, leading his own branch of nationalist Zionism, the New Zionist Organization, in 1935. Until his death he was commander of the Irgun, the underground Jewish military organization that operated in Palestine between 1937 and 1948. Jabotinsky's branch of Zionism believed in establishing a Jewish state in Palestine with the support of Jewish brigades, and the movement strongly advocated for Jewish self-defence and self-determination.

Jewish Immigrant Aid Society (JIAS) An organization that has provided a variety of services to Jewish immigrants to Canada from 1919 to the present. Its origins trace back to the first assembly of the Canadian Jewish Congress in 1919 when it was faced with a Jewish refugee crisis in Canada after World War I. In 1955 the organization changed its name to Jewish Immigrant Aid Services of Canada.

Judenrat (German, plural: Judenräte) Jewish Council. A group of Jewish leaders appointed by the Germans to administer and provide services to the local Jewish population under occupation and carry out German orders. The *Judenräte* appeared to be self-governing entities, but were under complete German control. The *Judenräte* faced difficult and complex moral decisions under brutal conditions and remain a contentious subject. The chairmen had to decide whether to comply or refuse to comply with German demands. Some were killed by the Nazis for refusing, while others committed suicide. Jewish officials who advocated compliance thought that cooperation might save at least some Jews. Some who denounced resistance efforts did so because they believed that armed resistance would bring death to the entire community.

Kaddish (Aramaic; holy) Also known as the Mourner's Prayer, Kaddish is said as part of mourning rituals in Jewish prayer services as well as at funerals and memorials.

kapo (German) A concentration camp prisoner appointed by the SS to oversee other prisoners as slave labourers.

keddoshim (Hebrew; holy ones) A word used to refer to the victims of the Holocaust. Its origins come from a reference to the mandate of *Kiddush Hashem*, which has several meanings, one of which refers to being killed for the act of sanctifying God and being Jewish. It is also the name of a portion in the Torah (in the seventh book of Leviticus).

Konzentrationslager (German; concentration camp). Often abbreviated as KZ.

kosher (Hebrew) Fit to eat according to Jewish dietary laws. Observant Jews follow a system of rules known as *kashruth* that regulates what can be eaten, how food is prepared and how meat and poultry are slaughtered. Food is kosher when it is deemed fit for consumption according to this system of rules. There are several foods that are forbidden, most notably pork products and shellfish.

Linz The third-largest city in Austria and capital of the state of Upper Austria (Oberösterreich). The concentration camp Mauthausen was approximately twenty-five kilometres from the city. One of the three main Austrian DP camps for Jewish refugees was established in the city of Linz-Bindermichl – the other two were Ebelsberg and Wegscheid.

Lubavitch A branch of Orthodox, Hasidic Judaism that was founded in Lyubavichi, Lithuania, in the late eighteenth century. The Lubavitch philosophy differs from other Hasidic branches in that it emphasizes intellectual over emotional reasoning.

Luftwaffe The German air force.

March of the Living Established in 1988, this annual event takes place in April on Holocaust Memorial Day (Yom HaShoah) in Poland and aims to educate primarily Jewish students and young adults from around the world about the Holocaust and Jewish life during World War II. Along with Holocaust survivors, participants march the three kilometres from Auschwitz to Birkenau to commemorate all who perished in the Holocaust. The concept of the March of the Living comes from the Nazi death marches that Jews were forced to go on when they were being evacuated from the forced labour and concentration camps at the very end of the war. Many Jews died during these marches, and thus the March of the Living was created to both remember and contrast this history, by celebrating Jewish life and strength. After spending time in Poland, participants travel to Israel and join in celebrations there for Israel's remembrance and independence days.

Mauthausen A notoriously brutal concentration camp, located about twenty kilometres east of the Austrian city of Linz. First established in 1936 shortly after the annexation of Austria to imprison "asocial" political opponents of the Third Reich, the camp grew to encompass fifty nearby subcamps and became the largest forced labour complex in German-occupied territory. By the end of the war, close to 200,000 prisoners had passed through the Mauthausen forced-labour camp system and almost 120,000 of them died there – including 38,120 Jews – from starvation, disease and hard labour. Mauthausen was classified as a Category 3 camp, which essentially meant that inmates were worked to death, often by the brutal work conditions in the Weiner-Graben stone quarry. The US army liberated the camp on May 5, 1945.

mensch (Yiddish) A good person, someone having honourable qualities; mensch generally refers to someone who is selfless or who has integrity.

mezuzah (Hebrew; literally: doorpost) The small piece of parchment inscribed with specific Hebrew texts from the Torah – usually enclosed in a decorative casing – that is placed on the doorframes of homes of observant Jews.

Mond, Bernard A Jewish general in the Polish army, Mond commanded the Polish 6th Infantry based in Krakow between 1932 and 1938. During World War II he was a prisoner of war in a German camp.

Nazi camps The Nazis established roughly 20,000 prison camps between 1933 and 1945. Although the term concentration camp is often used to refer generally to all these facilities, the various camps in fact served a wide variety of functions. They included concentration camps; forced labour camps; prisoner-of-war (POW) camps; transit camps; and death camps. Concentration camps were detention facilities first built in 1933 to imprison "enemies of the state," while forced labour camps held prisoners who had to do hard physical labour under brutal working conditions. POW camps were designated for captured prisoners of war and transit camps operated as holding facilities for Jews who were to be transported to main camps – often death camps in Poland. Death camps were killing centres where designated groups of people were murdered on a highly organized, mass scale. Some camps, such as Mauthausen, combined several of these functions into a huge complex of camps.

Oberscharführer (German; senior squad leader) A Nazi SS party rank between 1932 and 1945. *See also* SS.

Ordnungsdienst (German; literally: Order Service) The Jewish ghetto police force established by the Jewish Councils on the orders of the Germans. The force, who were armed with clubs, was created to carry out various tasks in the ghettos, such as traffic control and guarding the ghetto gates. Eventually, some policemen also participated in rounding up Jews for forced labour and transportation to the death camps. There has been much debate and controversy surrounding the role of the Jewish Councils and the Jewish police. Even though the Jewish police exercised considerable power within the ghetto, to the Germans these policemen were still Jews and subject to the same fate as other Jews.

ORT The Organization for Rehabilitation through Training was a vocational school system founded for Jews by Jews in Russia in 1880.

Orthodox Judaism The set of beliefs and practices of Jews for whom the strict observance of Jewish law is closely connected to faith; it is characterized by strict religious observance of Jewish dietary laws, restrictions on work on the Sabbath and holidays, and a modest code of dress.

OSS (Office of Strategic Services) The US intelligence unit established during World War II (1942–1945) that was the precursor to the CIA (Central Intelligence Agency).

partisans Members of irregular military forces or resistance movements formed to oppose armies of occupation. During World War II there were a number of different partisan groups that opposed both the Nazis and their collaborators in several countries. The term partisan could include highly organized, almost paramilitary groups such as the Soviet Red Army partisans; ad hoc groups bent more on survival than resistance; and roving groups of bandits who plundered what they could from all sides during the war. In Poland, the partisans were known as the Polish Underground State and the primary partisan group developed into the Armia Krajowa, the Polish Home Army.

peyes (Yiddish; Hebrew, *peyot*) Side-curls or earlocks. Among certain Orthodox Jewish communities, males refrain from cutting the hair at the edge of the face, in front of the ears. The practice of growing these distinctive locks of hair is based on a strict interpretation of the biblical verse "You shall not round off the side-growth of your head, or destroy the side-growth of your beard" (Leviticus XIX:27).

Pidyon HaBen (Hebrew; Redemption of the Son) A Jewish ritual performed one month after the birth of the firstborn son, in which parents symbolically redeem their infant from a Cohen (a descendant of the ancient Jewish priests); based on a biblical concept that firstborn males belong to God.

Płaszów The labour camp constructed on two Jewish cemeteries in a suburb of Krakow in 1942 and enlarged to become a concentration camp in January 1944. Płaszów was also used as a transit camp – more than 150,000 people passed through the camp, many en route to Auschwitz, and about 80,000 were murdered in the camp itself, from either execution or hard labour. By mid-1944, Płaszów held over 20,000 prisoners; inmates were used for slave labour in the quarry or railway construction and were subject to the volatile whims of camp commandant Amon Göth, who was personally responsible for more than 8,000 deaths. *See also* Göth, Amon.

Polish-British Common Defence Pact Also called the Anglo French Assurance Pact. On March 31, 1939, Britain and France guaranteed to defend Poland's independence, and the pact, signed on August 25, assured mutual military support in the event of invasion by a European power. There was an additional secret clause that specified Germany as the "European power" and the pact was signed by both countries in an effort to halt Germany's expansion and protect Poland after Germany invaded Czechoslovakia in March 1939. After the pact was signed, Hitler delayed the invasion of Poland from August 26 to September 1.

Purim (Hebrew; literally: lots) The celebration of the Jews' escape from annihilation in Persia. The story is that Haman, advisor to the King of Persia, planned to exterminate the Jews, but his plot was foiled by Queen Esther and her cousin Mordecai, who convinced the king to save them. Purim, during which people masquerade as one of the figures in the Purim story, is celebrated with parades, costumes and a retelling of the story. *See also* Adloyada.

Pustków-Dębica A labour camp that was originally built in 1940 to house an SS training facility. The camp initially held mainly Jewish prisoners, but after 1941 the camp population also included Soviet prisoners of war; in 1942, the facility expanded to incarcerate Polish forced-labourers as well. Inmates in Pustków built rockets for the Nazi war machine. Conditions were harsh in the camp and an estimated 15,000 prisoners died or were killed there.

Rassenschande (German; literally: racial shame, racial pollution) A term used during the Third Reich to denote forbidden contact between Jews and "Aryans" that specifically forbade marriage or sexual relations, which was outlawed as part of the Nazi racial laws (particularly the September 15, 1935, "Law for the Protection of German Blood and Honour").

Reform Judaism Also known as Progressive Judaism, Reform Judaism emerged in nineteenth-century Germany in response to the previous century's rise in secularism in Europe, the Haskalah (Jewish Enlightenment) and Jewish emancipation, which allowed Jews more social and economic freedom. The Reform movement introduced a variety of changes in Jewish observance, including incorporating the local language into religious services in place of, or in addition to, Hebrew.

Reichstag The German parliament.

Revisionist Zionism One of several competing strains of Zionism that emerged in the decades prior to the establishment of the State of Israel. It was founded on the philosophy of Jewish statehood in Palestine. The Revisionists also believed that military and political power ultimately determined the fate of peoples and nations and focused on the need for Jewish self-defence. *See also* Zionism; Zionist and Jewish movements in interwar Poland.

Rosh Hashanah (Hebrew) New Year. The autumn holiday that marks the beginning of the Jewish year and ushers in the High Holy Days. It is observed by a synagogue service that ends with blowing the *shofar* (horn), which marks the beginning of the holiday. The service is usually followed by a family dinner where traditional and symbolic foods are eaten. *See also* Yom Kippur.

Sabbath/Shabbat (Hebrew; in Yiddish, Shabbes, Shabbos) The weekly day of rest beginning Friday at sunset and ending Saturday at sundown ushered in by the lighting of candles on Friday night and the recitation of blessings over wine and challah (braided egg bread); a day of celebration as well as prayer, it is customary to eat three festive meals, attend synagogue services and refrain from doing any work or travelling.

Schindler, Oskar (1908–1974) German businessman who saved the lives of more than 1,000 Jews, who are often referred to as *Schindlerjuden* (Schindler's Jews). Schindler, a member of the Nazi party, took over an enamel factory situated close to the Płaszów labour camp in 1940 and began employing Jewish workers there, sheltering them from the harsh conditions at the camp. Though Schindler profited from the cheap labour, he was increasingly motivated to preserve the lives of his workers and went to extreme lengths to save them from death, often advocating for them and bribing camp commandant Amon Göth and other Nazi officials who came to inspect the factory. Schindler used his own funds to construct a subcamp at his enamel factory to ensure the safety and nourishment of his workers as well as close to 450 workers from nearby factories. He was twice arrested for black market activity but used his influence to escape the charges. When his enamel factory, Emalia, was forced to close in 1944 as the Soviet troops advanced, he heroically rescued more than 1,000 Jews from deportation to Auschwitz by declaring them to be "essential to the war effort" and transporting them to his new ammunitions factory in Brünnlitz, Sudetenland. Oskar Schindler was awarded the honoured title of Righteous Among the Nations by Yad Vashem in 1993 and was the subject of Steven Spielberg's 1993 film *Schindler's List*, based on the novel *Schindler's Ark* by Thomas Keneally.

shegetz A non-Jewish male. The Hebrew origin of the word is "sheketz," meaning "impurity." Modern usage of the term to refer to gentiles can be either humorous or derogatory, depending on the context.

shiksa A non-Jewish female. *See also* shegetz.

shoyket (Yiddish; in Hebrew, *shochet*) Ritual slaughterer. A man conversant with the religious teaching of *kashruth*, trained to slaughter animals painlessly and to check that the product meets the various criteria of kosher slaughter. *See also* kosher.

shtreimel A fur-rimmed hat worn by Hasidic Jews on the Sabbath and other major Jewish holidays.

shul (Yiddish) Synagogue or Jewish house of prayer.

simcha (Hebrew; gladness, joy) Generally refers to a festive occasion.

social order in Nazi camps Many Nazi camps had populations that included a variety of non-Jewish prisoners – such as political offenders, communists, homosexuals, or common criminals from Germany and German-occupied Europe. The camp administrators – the SS *Totenkopfverbände* (Death's Head Unit, who wore a skull-and-crossbones insignia on their lapels as well as on their caps) – maintained a strict hierarchy that pitted one group of prisoners against another, giving privileges to those at the top of the hierarchy and meting out brutal punishment to those at the bottom. Each group in the Nazi camp organization was clearly identified by a complex classification system using combinations of triangle badges of different colours and markings. The camps were run by the SS and ultimate authority within the camp rested entirely with the SS *Kommandant*. Below the *Kommandant* were various other staff, including the camp guards and the *Blockführer*, who were responsible for the administration of individual barracks. Camp authorities also gave prisoners from higher-ranking groups limited authority to help control the rest of the prisoners. These "privileged" prisoners, called kapos, or barracks supervisors, were often vicious in their treatment of fellow inmates who were below them in status.

SS The abbreviation for Schutzstaffel (Defence Corps). The SS was established in 1925 as Adolf Hitler's elite corps of personal bodyguards. Under the directorship of its leader, Heinrich Himmler, its membership grew from 280 in 1929 to 50,000 when the Nazis came to power in 1933 and nearly a quarter of a million on the eve of World War II. The SS was comprised of the Allgemeine-SS (General SS) and the Waffen-SS (Armed, or Combat SS). The General SS dealt with policing and the enforcement of Nazi racial policies in Germany and the Nazi-occupied countries. An important unit within the SS was the Reichssicherheitshauptamt (RSHA, the Central Office of Reich Security), whose responsibility included the Gestapo (Geheime Staatspolizei). The SS ran the forced labour, concentration and death camps, with all their associated economic enterprises, and also fielded its own Waffen-SS military divisions, including some recruited from the occupied countries.

Sudetenland The western border region of former Czechoslovakia that was inhabited primarily by ethnic Germans before World War II. In an attempt to prevent World War II, Britain, France and Italy agreed to the annexation of the Sudetenland by the Third Reich as part of the Munich Agreement, which was signed on September 30, 1938.

Treblinka A labour and death camp created as part of Operation Reinhard, the German code word for the Nazi plan for the mass extermination of European Jews. A slave-labour camp (Treblinka I) was built in November 1941 near the villages of Treblinka and Makinia Górna, about eighty kilometres northeast of Warsaw in Poland. Treblinka II, the killing centre, was constructed in a sparsely populated and heavily wooded area about 1.5 kilometres from the labour camp. From July 1942 to October 1943 more than 750,000 Jews were killed at Treblinka, making it second only to Auschwitz in the numbers of Jews killed. Treblinka I and II were both liberated by the Soviet army in July 1944.

treif Food that is not allowed under Jewish dietary laws. *See also* kosher.

Ukrainische Hilfspolizei (German) Ukrainian Auxiliary Police. The Ukrainian Auxiliary Police was formed in the wake of the German occupation of eastern Poland and the Ukraine in June 1941 and actively collaborated with the Nazis in the implementation of their plans to persecute and eventually mass murder Jews. The Ukrainian Auxiliary Police escorted Jews to forced labour sites, guarded the ghettos and engaged in mass-murder shooting operations.

United Nations Relief and Rehabilitation Administration (UNRRA) An organization created at a 44-nation conference in Washington, DC on November 9, 1943, to provide economic assistance to Nazi-occupied European nations following World War II and to repatriate and assist war refugees

Wehrmacht (German) The Germany army.

Yiddish A language derived from Middle High German with elements of Hebrew, Aramaic, Romance and Slavic languages, and written in Hebrew characters. There are similarities between Yiddish and contemporary German.

Yom Kippur (Hebrew; literally "day of atonement") A solemn day of fasting and repentance that comes eight days after Rosh Hashanah, the Jewish New Year, and marks the end of the high holidays. *See also* Rosh Hashanah.

zaida (Yiddish; also zeyde, zeide) Grandfather.

Zionism A movement promoted by the Viennese Jewish journalist Theodor Herzl, who argued in his 1896 book *Der Judenstaat* (The Jewish State) that the best way to resolve the problem of antisemitism and persecution of Jews in Europe was to create an independent Jewish state in the historic Jewish homeland of Biblical Israel. Zionists promoted the revival of Hebrew as a Jewish national language. In interwar Poland, Zionism was one of many Jewish political parties with affiliated schools and youth groups. *See also* Revisionist Zionism.

Zionist and Jewish movements in interwar Poland Among the significant Jewish political movements that flourished in Poland before World War II were various Zionist parties – the General Zionists; the Labour Zionists (Poale Zion); the Revisionist Zionists formed under Ze'ev Jabotinsky; and the Orthodox Religious Zionists (the Mizrachi movement) – and the entirely secular and socialist Jewish Workers' Alliance, known as the Bund. Although Zionism and Bundism were both Jewish national movements and served as Jewish political parties in interwar Poland, Zionism advocated a Jewish national homeland in the Land of Israel, while Bundism advocated Jewish cultural autonomy in the Diaspora. A significant number of Polish Jews in the interwar years preferred to affiliate with the non-Zionist religious Orthodox party, Agudath Israel, that advocated political orthodoxy. *See also* Bund; Revisionist Zionism; and Zionism.

Photographs

1 (Top left) Willie Sterner's father, Hersz Leib Sterner, as a soldier in the Russian army during World War I, circa 1915.

2 Willie's mother, Hinda Reizel Sterner, circa 1921.

3 Hinda Reizel Sterner with Willie's brother Abraham and sister Ida at the spa where Hinda Sterner went for treatments for her arthritis. Busko-Zdrój, 1928.

1 Willie Sterner, at age nineteen, with his family not long before the war. Left to right (behind) Willie; Willie's mother, Hinda; his father, Hersz; and his brother, Josel Meier, age sixteen; (in front) Willie's sisters; Ida, age twelve; Rachel, age nine; Sarah, age six; Genia, age eleven; and his brother Abraham, age fourteen. Krakow, 1938.

2 Willie at work for his father's contracting company, Fine Home Painting, Decorating and Sign Painting. Krakow, 1938.

3 Willie as the goalie for the Gwiazda Jewish soccer team, which was part of the Zionist Poale Zion organization's sports club. Krakow, 1938.

1 Willie (left) with his friend Leon Monderer (centre) and another friend on the
   Vistula River. Krakow, 1938.

2 Willie (second from the left) with his friends Ida (far left), Sarah (second from
   the right) and Leon outside the Wawel Palace. Krakow, 1938.

1 Willie (fourth from the right) during his first summer at pre-military school. Krakow, 1938.

2 Willie (left) during his second summer at pre-military school. Krakow, 1939.

1 Willie (second from the left) with his friend Ida (third from the left); his girlfriend, Helen (second from the right); and Leon (far right). Krakow, 1938.

2 Willie and some of his friends during the war wearing armbands that identify
them as Jews. Left to right: Joseph, Helen, Willie and Rosie. Krakow, 1940.

SOKOŁOWSKA MARIA &
WŁADYSŁAW
SOKOŁOWSKI CHILDREN: WIESŁAW
& KRYSTYNA
STEINDL PAULINA
"STRZAŁKA KAZIMIERA"
SZOSTAK STANISŁAW
SZTETNER EDWARD
SZWAJ JAN & JULIANNA
SZYMAŃSKI ROMUALD &
JADWIGA

1 Kazimiera (Kazia) Strzalka, Willie's friend and neighbour from Wolbrom who gave him shelter and then helped him when he was in the Rakowice forced labour camp. Wolbrom, 1941. She also gave him the precious photos of his family in this book.

2 Kazimiera Strzalka's name inscribed on one of the walls of the Garden of the Righteous Among the Nations at Yad Vashem, the Holocaust Martyrs' and Heroes' Remembrance Authority in Jerusalem. Kazimiera Strzalka is the only person from Wolbrom to be awarded the title of Righteous Among the Nations by Yad Vashem.

The Schindler enamel factory, Deutsche Emailwaren Fabrik (DEF) at 4 Lipowa Street in the Zabłocie district of Krakow. (Photo courtesy of Noa Cafri)

1 Willie (standing, centre) with the Jewish police force in the Lichteneck Displaced
   Persons camp. Wels, Austria, 1945.

2 Willie (right) with Stefan, a US soldier, at the Lichteneck DP camp. Wels, 1945.

3 Willie (right) at the Bindermichl DP camp. Linz, Austria, 1946.

4 Willie and Eva at the Imperial Villa of Emperor Franz Jozef I not long after their
   wedding. Bad Ischl, Austria, 1946.

COMMUNITY BINDERMICHL	KOMITEE BINDERMICHL

Name: Sterner Wili

Home: Bindermichl

Place: Chief   Police

Born: 15/9. 1919.

OFFICER, POLICE FORCE
This is to certify that Sterner Wili
has authority to enforce law and order at camp Bindermichl as laid down by Commander.

Leon D. Gladding

Signed by Commander

LEON D. GLADDING
Lt. Col. INFANTRY
COMMANDING

Obige Kommandantur bescheinigt, daß

Sterner   Wili

als   Chef Police   Dienst leistet;

Bindermichl 19 6-6/7/48

Kommandantur

3

1   Willie in his uniform as chief of the Jewish police for the Bindermichl DP camp. Linz, Austria, 1946.

2   Willie (centre) proudly marching with members of the Jewish police force. Salzburg, Austria, 1946.

3   Willie's identification card as chief of the Jewish police. Linz, 1946.

The Linz-Bindermichl Jewish police force. The painting of Willie in the centre at the top is a self-portrait. Linz, 1946.

1 Willie (right) and Leon Green (left) in Dachau to testify at the war crimes trials, 1947.

2 Willie (back row, second from the right) with the group of refugees that came from the DP camp in Linz-Bindermichl to testify at the Dachau war crimes trials. 1947.

3 (bottom left) Eva Sterner (left) and fellow refugee Bella Piler at a memorial service in Gunskirchen, standing beside the monument put up to commemorate the Jews who died in the camp; (bottom right) Eva (left), Willie (centre) and Bella in front of the monument. Gunskirchen, 1947.

1

2

3

1 Eva and Willie on the train from Salzberg, Austria to Bremerhaven, Germany on their way to Canada, 1948.

2 Willie as a member of the military police on board the military transport ship, uss *General M.B. Stewart*, that took him and Eva to Canada, 1948.

3 Landing in Halifax on the eve of Rosh Hashanah 1948.

1 Harry Sterner's bar mitzvah at Young Israel of Val Royal synagogue. Montreal, 1965.

2 Abie Sterner's bar mitzvah at Young Israel of Val Royal synagogue. Montreal, 1969.

3 Willie and Eva dancing at a celebration. Montreal, 1970.

4 Willie in his tobacco shop. Montreal, 1982.

1 Willie at the monument to the victims on the site of the Płaszów forced labour camp during the March of the Living. Krakow, 2000.

2 The monument on the site of the former Treblinka death camp that commemorates, among others, Jewish victims from Wolbrom. Małkinia Górna, Poland, 2000.

3 Willie and Eva (second row, middle) with the March of the Living group at Płaszów, 2000.

Painting by the author of the Warsaw Ghetto Uprising.

1　The Sterner family. Left to right (starting with the bottom left): Willie's great-granddaughter Kaylay (seated); his son Harry's daughter Melanie; his son Abie's daughter Seana; Harry; Abie's daughter (and Kaylay's mother), Patricia; Harry's daughter Jessica; Willie; his son Abie; and Eva. Montreal, 2005.

2　Willie Sterner with his family. Left to right (behind): Harry Sterner; Harry's daughter Melanie; Harry's daughter Jessica; Abie Sterner's wife, Nicole; and Willie; (seated in front): Abie's daughter Patricia; Abie's daughter Seana; and Eva. Montreal, 2005.

Eva's Story

My name is Eva Sterner (née Mrowka). I was born on November 11, 1925, in Sosnowiec, in southern Poland. I am the only survivor of my family of five.

My parents were Abraham and Raizel (née Chmielewski); my father, who passed away before the war, was a butcher. I was the youngest of three children – only fourteen when World War II began. My brother, Izchak, born in 1917, was twenty-two when the Nazis invaded Poland; his wife, Sala, was nineteen. Next came my sister, Gita, who was eighteen in 1939.

Growing up in Sosnowiec, I was a happy and healthy young girl with lots of good friends. I attended public school and was a member of the Zionist organization HaNoar HaOved ("the working youth"). We had a good life.

Our tragedy began on September 1, 1939, when the Nazis occupied our city and brought terror and mass murder. They waged a war against an innocent, unarmed Jewish population whose only crime was being Jewish. They humiliated and degraded us, and seized our businesses and all our valuables. From that point on, Jews had to work for the Nazis for no money and it was very hard to get food. The Nazis also brought in many restrictions: we were no longer allowed to travel on public transportation; our schools were closed; we couldn't go to movie theatres or walk on the beach. We weren't even allowed to walk on the sidewalk – we had to walk in the middle of the street. We had to wear armbands with the Star of David so that the Nazis could identify us from far away. Any Jew who wasn't wearing an armband was killed on the spot. Jewish professionals were forbidden to use their titles and couldn't work in their professions. Rabbis were no longer allowed to pray with members of their synagogue – the Nazis refused to recognize the title of "rabbi."

Between 1941 and 1943 I worked at forced labour in Sosnowiec, making Nazi uniforms for the Hans Held company. It was hard work; we were under constant pressure and always hungry. In the fall of 1942, we were forced to move into the ghetto in Srodula, a very poor district of the city.[1]

In 1943, I was sent to the forced labour camp Lilienthal in Germany and then to the Nordhausen camp, a subcamp of the Dora-Mittelbau concentration camp. In both places, the conditions were terrible. In 1944, I was sent to the notoriously brutal forced labour camp in Mauthausen, Austria. This was beyond anything I had ever experienced – Mauthausen was a camp of mass destruction, a death camp in which the crematorium operated twenty-four hours a day. There was no break from the smell of burning human flesh.

Near the end of 1944, a large group of Jews from the camp were sent on a forced march to the terrible camp in Gunskirchen, Austria. Many people were killed by the Nazis on that march because, weak and exhausted, they couldn't walk fast enough. It was on this walk that I met a young man by the name Willie, from Krakow. In the few minutes that we could talk, I asked him if he knew anything about my family. Unfortunately, we had to part quickly because a Nazi guard was approaching – the prisoners weren't allowed to talk to each other on this forced march.

---

1   The ghetto in Srodula was established in the fall 1942 and by March 1943, 14,000 Jews from Sosnowiec and the surrounding area had been moved there. Deportations to Auschwitz began in June 1943 and by August 9, 1943, the ghetto had been entirely liquidated.

After what seemed like an eternity, we arrived in Gunskirchen, a horrible, dirty camp. There was no work there, but also no food. Lying on the ground outside the barracks were dozens of corpses. Life in Gunskirchen was a living nightmare and none of us expected to survive it. Then, on May 5, 1945, we were liberated by the US army. Suddenly, we were free, happy to be alive and hoping against hope that some of our relatives had survived. Many people had survived but never made it out of the barracks; they were too weak and died after liberation. It was heartbreaking that they survived the Nazis only to die before they could experience freedom.

I contracted typhoid fever and was sent to a German hospital. It took about two months for me to recover and at that point I went to the Displaced Persons' camp Lichteneck in Wels, Austria. I went to Wels because many of my friends were already there. All my girl-friends were so happy to see me when I arrived that we all laughed and talked at once. Then I looked around and saw a young man I recognized from the forced march from Mauthausen to Gunskirchen. I remembered his name and called out, "Hi, Willie." He was really shocked to hear me call him by name, but I reminded him about where we had met. He was very happy to see me alive. He hadn't recognized me because on that march my face had been so dirty and I was wearing such filthy rags. We became good friends. He was all alone and I didn't have any family either. Not long after Willie and I got re-acquainted, he received a very special guest in the camp – none other than Oskar Schindler. Schindler was pleased to see that Willie had me as a close friend. He didn't look any better than a DP, but Willie was so glad to see him; he was Willie's hero.

In the spring of 1946, Willie and I both moved to the DP community of Bindermichl in Linz. There were Jewish refugees from all over Europe – from Hungary, Poland, Romania, France and Czechoslovakia – as well as some partisans. It was a wonderful mixture of people and we formed a very close-knit community, but our lives were still not the same as they had been before the war. We missed our loved ones terribly. Still, we were safe in Linz-Bindermichl and we got lots of help from Jewish organizations from the USA and Canada and from the United Nations Relief and Rehabilitation Administration (UNRRA). I was grateful for their help.

Willie and I were married on July 16, 1946, in Salzburg, Austria. We had a lovely wedding under a chuppah (canopy), officiated by an Orthodox rabbi and with lots of good friends, two Jewish chaplains from the US army, some of the Jewish committee members and a few Jewish police officers. It was a very nice simcha (celebration), but it was hard not to feel the absence of family.

In October 1948, we had an opportunity to move to Canada. We arrived in Halifax, Nova Scotia with no money, no family and no friends; we didn't even speak any English. But we got generous help from Jewish organizations; we will always be grateful for everything they did to help us. We didn't have much, but compared to where we had come from, Canada was a haven. We settled in Montreal, found work and we built up a small family. We have two fine sons, Harry and Abie, and they have given us the joy of wonderful grandchildren.

When we retired, Willie and I fulfilled our dream and went to Israel for four weeks. What a beautiful small country! We are very proud of Israel.

Now that he is retired, Willie works at the Montreal Holocaust Centre, educating people about the Holocaust. He has been interviewed on television and has travelled on speaking engagements within Canada and in the United States. In Montreal he speaks at synagogues, colleges and high schools. We spent the winters in Miami Beach, Florida, where Willie worked at the Holocaust Documentation and Education Center, speaking to young people from high schools, colleges, universities, churches and synagogues. It isn't easy for Willie to speak about what he has been through, but he feels that it is his duty as a Holocaust survivor to tell the world what happened to us while the world was silent. I went with Willie when he was invited to speak at a very important gathering of about six hundred children of survivors in Detroit. Our two sons came as well, to support Willie. I have travelled with Willie to a number of other places where he was invited to speak, including to the Jewish Federation Campaign in Nashville, Tennessee.

Willie and I both went through a terrible tragedy – we lost the best part of our lives in such a brutal way. We survivors cannot forget the terrible slaughter of innocent Jewish families. We still always suffer from the Holocaust and the loss of our loved ones. I hope the leaders of the world will think about the future and, if a maniac like Hitler comes again, they stop him before it's too late. It's impossible to understand how we survived such horror. We act normal but it's always with us; we still dream about it every night.

Index

The Azrieli Foundation was established in 1989 to realize and extend the philanthropic vision of David J. Azrieli, C.M., C.Q., M.Arch. The Foundation's mission is to support a wide spectrum of initiatives in education and research. The Azrieli Foundation is an active supporter of programs in the fields of Jewish education, the education of architects, scientific and medical research, and education in the arts. The Azrieli Foundation's many well-known initiatives include: the Holocaust Survivor Memoirs Program, which collects, preserves, publishes and distributes the written memoirs of survivors in Canada; the Azrieli Institute for Educational Empowerment, an innovative program successfully working to keep at-risk youth in school; and the Azrieli Fellows Program, which promotes academic excellence and leadership on the graduate level at Israeli universities.